MAURITIUS

TRAVEL GUIDE

2023

Mauritius Travel Treasures: Immerse Yourself in the Island's Magic" An Insider's Guide to Must-See Attractions, Captivating Beaches, Tropical Flavors, and Timeless Elegance

By

ROY ORTIZ

TABLE OF CONTENT

My Mauritius Vacation Experience

I recently had the incredible opportunity to spend a vacation in Mauritius, and I must say it was an unforgettable experience. I was captivated by the natural beauty, warm hospitality, and rich cultural heritage of this beautiful island from the moment I set foot on it.

My adventure began in Port Louis, Mauritius' vibrant capital city. I was immersed in the vibrant sights, sounds, and aromas of the local markets as I strolled through the bustling streets. I couldn't help but indulge in some delectable street food, savoring the flavors of traditional Mauritian cuisine. The food's blend of Indian, Chinese, African, and European influences was a culinary delight.

Exploring the beautiful beaches was a highlight of my vacation. Belle Mare Beach, with its pristine white sand and crystal-clear turquoise waters, took my breath away. I spent hours lying in the sun, enjoying the gentle ocean breeze, and occasionally diving into the cool waves. Snorkeling in the Blue Bay Marine Park was an absolute delight, as I marveled at the vibrant coral reefs and the colorful marine life that called them home.

Hiking in Black River Gorges National Park was one of my most memorable experiences. The lush greenery, cascading waterfalls, and diverse wildlife made me feel like I'd stepped into a tropical paradise. I hiked the trails, taking in the sights and sounds of nature. The panoramic views from the viewpoints were breathtaking, making the trek worthwhile.

I also had the opportunity to learn about the local culture and traditions. I went to the Pamplemousses Botanical Garden, where I marveled at the vast collection of exotic plants and the famous giant water lilies. I saw a lively Sega dance performance, where the infectious beats and colorful costumes brought Mauritian culture to life.

To truly unwind, I went to the Chamarel Colored Earths, a natural phenomenon in which the sands display a kaleidoscope of colors. It was a surreal sight that left me in awe of nature's wonders. I also relaxed at a luxurious spa resort, where I received rejuvenating massages and wellness treatments that left me feeling refreshed and revitalized.

The Mauritian people treated me with warmth and friendliness throughout my vacation. Their genuine hospitality and willingness to share their culture and traditions made my trip even more memorable. I made wonderful memories and lasting connections with both fellow travelers and locals.

As I bid farewell to this paradise island, I couldn't help but be grateful for the incredible experiences and memories I had made. Mauritius truly exceeded my expectations in every way. It is a destination that combines natural beauty, adventure, relaxation, and cultural immersion. My Mauritius vacation will always have a special place in my heart, and I can't wait to return and create more treasured memories in this enchanting paradise.

Introduction to Mauritius

Mauritius is a small island country in the Indian Ocean, off the southeast coast of Africa. It is well-known for its breathtaking natural beauty, pristine beaches, and rich cultural heritage. Mauritius is made up of the main island as well as several smaller islands such as Rodrigues, Agalega, and the Cargados Carajos Shoals.

Throughout its history, Mauritius has been colonized by the Dutch, French, and British. It gained independence from Britain in 1968 and became a republic in 1992. The country is a member of the Commonwealth of Nations and has a parliamentary democracy.

Mauritius is known as the "Pearl of the Indian Ocean" because of its beautiful landscapes, crystal-clear waters, and vibrant coral reefs. Its tropical climate, with warm and pleasant temperatures all year, makes it a popular tourist destination for those looking for sun, sea, and adventure.

Mauritius' multiculturalism is one of its distinguishing characteristics. The population is made up of people from various ethnic groups, including Indians, Africans, Chinese, and Europeans. This cultural diversity is reflected in the cuisine, languages, festivals, and traditions of the country. Although English, French, and Mauritian Creole are the official languages, a sizable portion of the population also speaks Hindi, Bhojpuri, Tamil, and other languages.

Tourism, along with textiles, sugar, financial services, and information technology, is critical to the Mauritius economy. To cater to its growing tourism industry, the country has invested in developing a strong infrastructure, including world-class hotels, resorts, and golf courses.

Aside from its beautiful beaches, Mauritius has a variety of activities and attractions for visitors. Water sports such as snorkeling, scuba diving, kiteboarding, and deep-sea fishing are available to thrill seekers. The lush interior of the island is dotted with national parks and nature reserves, providing opportunities for hiking, birdwatching, and exploring the island's unique flora and fauna. Mauritius has a rich history and cultural heritage as well. Visitors can learn about the island's history of sugar plantations and the abolition of slavery by exploring colonial architecture and visiting museums. Local crafts, textiles, spices, and souvenirs can be found at the vibrant street markets and shopping centers.

In conclusion, Mauritius is a tropical paradise known for its breathtaking natural beauty, cultural diversity, and friendly people. Mauritius is a memorable destination for travelers from all over the world, whether they are looking for relaxation on pristine beaches, thrilling water sports, or immersing themselves in a vibrant cultural experience.

A. Geographical Location Of Mauritius

Mauritius is located in the southwestern Indian Ocean, approximately 2,000 kilometers (1,200 miles) off the African continent's southeast coast. It lies between the latitudes of 19°58'S and 20°31'S and the longitudes of 57°18'E and 57°49'E.

The Mascarene Islands, which also include Rodrigues, Agalega, and the Cargados Carajos Shoals, comprise the island nation. Mauritius is the largest island in the group, spanning approximately 2,040 square kilometers (790 square miles).

The island of Réunion, a French overseas department, is located to the east of Mauritius. Madagascar, located about 870 kilometers (540 miles) to the west, is the closest mainland.

Mauritius is distinguished by its volcanic origin, with mountains and plateaus dominating the central part of the island. Piton de la Petite Rivière Noire, at 828 meters (2,717 feet) above sea level, is the highest point.

Mauritius' coastline features beautiful sandy beaches and is surrounded by coral reefs that protect it from the open ocean. Several offshore islands and islets, such as Île aux Cerfs and Coin de Mire, add to the country's scenic appeal.

Overall, Mauritius has a strategic location in the Indian Ocean, providing a tropical paradise with stunning landscapes, clear turquoise waters, and an abundance of marine life.

B. Weather and Climate

Mauritius has a tropical climate that is distinguished by warm temperatures all year. The surrounding Indian Ocean, which moderates the temperature and provides moisture, influences the weather.

The country has two distinct seasons: a warm and humid summer season that lasts from November to April, and a cooler and drier winter season that lasts from May to October.

During the summer, temperatures along the coast range from 25°C to 33°C (77°F to 91°F), while the interior can be slightly cooler. The humidity is higher, and thunderstorms and rain are more common, especially in the afternoon and evening. This is also cyclone season, with tropical cyclones potentially affecting the region between December and April.

Mauritius' winter season is mild, with temperatures ranging from 18°C to 25°C (64°F to 77°F) along the coast. The humidity is lower, and the weather is mostly sunny and pleasant. Rainfall is less common during this period, and sea temperatures remain warm, making it ideal for swimming and other water activities.

Mauritius has a pleasant climate for tourism all year. Summer brings warmer temperatures and the opportunity to enjoy water sports, whereas winter brings comfortable weather for outdoor activities and exploring the island's natural beauty. It is important to note that weather patterns can change, so before planning a trip, check local forecasts and weather updates.

C. History and Culture

Mauritius' rich and diverse history has shaped its distinct culture. The story of the island begins with the arrival of the Austronesian people around 2,000 years ago. Arab and Malay sailors arrived in Mauritius over time.

The Portuguese were the first Europeans to arrive in Mauritius in the 16th century, but they did not establish a permanent settlement. In 1598, the Dutch arrived and named the island after Prince Maurice of Nassau. Even though their colony was brief, they introduced sugarcane and deer to the island.

The French claimed Mauritius in 1715 and turned it into a prosperous colony. Sugarcane plantations flourished, and African slaves were brought to the island to work on them. The language, culture, and architecture of Mauritius have all been influenced by French rule.

During the Napoleonic Wars, the British took control of Mauritius in 1810. The sugar industry thrived under British rule, and indentured laborers were brought from India and other parts of the world to work on the plantations. The abolition of slavery in 1835 was a watershed moment in the island's history.

Mauritius gained independence from the British Commonwealth in 1968 and became a republic in 1992. Over the years, the island has maintained political stability and experienced consistent economic growth.

Mauritian culture is a vibrant fusion of Indian, African, Chinese, and European influences. As a result of this multicultural society, there is a diverse cultural landscape that celebrates its various ethnic groups.

Language is very important in Mauritian culture. The official language is English, but French and Mauritian Creole are widely spoken. Languages such as Hindi, Bhojpuri, Tamil, and Chinese dialects are also widely spoken in various communities.

Mauritius' cuisine reflects its diverse heritage. Traditional dishes contain elements of Indian, African, Chinese, and French cuisine. Popular culinary delights include spices, seafood, curries, samosas, biryani, and dholl puri (a type of flatbread).

Mauritian culture is based on music and dance. Sega is a traditional music genre with African and Malagasy influences that is distinguished by rhythmic beats and lively dance movements. Commonly used instruments include the ravanne (a drum), maravane (a shaker), and triangle.

Festivals are enthusiastically celebrated in Mauritius. The major festivals observed include Diwali, Eid, Chinese New Year, and Christmas, reflecting the island's multicultural fabric.

Mauritius' historical heritage has been preserved through colonial-era structures such as the Château de Labourdonnais and the Maison Eureka. Museums such as the Aapravasi Ghat and the Blue Penny Museum provide information about the island's history and cultural legacy.

The Mauritian people are well-known for their warm hospitality. Visitors to Mauritius frequently report feelings of inclusion and harmony in the multicultural society.

Mauritius' history and culture have shaped a diverse and welcoming society in which various traditions, languages, and customs coexist peacefully. Mauritius is a captivating destination that offers both historical insights and unforgettable experiences due to its rich cultural tapestry and the island's breathtaking natural beauty.

Chapter 1: Planning Your Trip To Mauritius

A. Best Time to Visit Mauritius

Mauritius is best visited during the shoulder seasons, which are May to June and September to November. During these times, the weather is generally pleasant, with moderate temperatures, lower humidity levels, and fewer chances of rain. The island is less crowded, allowing visitors to enjoy a more tranquil and relaxed experience.

Mauritius' autumn season lasts from May to June. Temperatures along the coast range from around 20°C to 25°C (68°F to 77°F), making it suitable for outdoor activities. The sea is still warm, making it ideal for swimming and water sports. This time of year also offers clear skies and fewer chances of rain.

The spring season in Mauritius lasts from September to November. Temperatures begin to rise, ranging from 22°C to 28°C (72°F to 82°F) along the coast. The humidity levels are lower compared to the summer months, and the weather is generally sunny and pleasant. This time is ideal for exploring the island's natural beauty, participating in outdoor activities, and relaxing on the beaches.

It is important to note that Mauritius has a tropical climate, and weather conditions can vary. The summer season, which lasts from November to April, brings warmer temperatures, higher humidity, and the possibility of tropical cyclones, especially from December to April. While visiting during the summer can still be enjoyable, it is best to stay up-to-date on weather forecasts and plan outdoor activities accordingly.

The winter season, from July to August, is cooler and drier, with temperatures ranging from 18°C to 25°C (64°F to 77°F) along the coast. Although it is considered the "off-peak" tourist season, it is still a popular time to visit Mauritius, especially for those seeking a more laid-back and peaceful vacation.

Finally, the best time to visit Mauritius depends on your preferences and the activities you intend to participate in. Whether you visit during the shoulder seasons or other months, Mauritius is a tropical paradise with a variety of attractions to enjoy all year.

B. Visa and Entry Requirements

The requirements for a visa and entry into Mauritius vary depending on your nationality and the purpose of your visit. Here is some general information about visiting Mauritius and obtaining a visa:

Visa-Free Entry: Citizens of many countries are permitted to enter Mauritius without a visa and stay for a set period of time. Depending on your nationality, this can last anywhere from 30 to 90 days. The United States, Canada, the United Kingdom, European Union member states, Australia, and New Zealand are among the visa-free countries. It's critical to double-check the duration of your visa-free entry and any additional requirements based on your nationality.

Visa on Arrival: Citizens of some countries who do not have visa-free entry into Mauritius can obtain a visa on arrival. This allows you to obtain a visa upon arrival at Mauritius' airport or seaport. The visa on arrival is typically valid for 60 days, but it is critical to confirm this information ahead of time to ensure you meet the requirements.

Pre-Arranged Visa: If you are a national of a country that requires a visa in advance, you must apply for one at the nearest Mauritian embassy or consulate before your trip. Typically, the application process entails submitting the necessary documents, which include a completed application form, passport photos, proof of accommodation, return flight tickets, and proof of sufficient funds.

It's important to note that visa requirements can change, so check with the nearest Mauritian embassy or consulate, or visit the official website of the Passport and Immigration Office of Mauritius, for the most up-to-date and accurate information on visa and entry requirements.

Furthermore, your passport must be valid for at least six months beyond your intended stay in Mauritius. Some travelers may also be required to show proof of medical insurance covering their stay.

Please keep in mind that the information provided here is only a general overview, and specific requirements may differ depending on your nationality and the purpose of your visit. Before traveling to Mauritius, it is best to seek personalized and accurate visa advice from the relevant authorities or professional advisors.

C. Currency and Money Matters

Mauritius' currency is the Mauritian Rupee (MUR). Here is some information about money and currency in Mauritius:

Currency Exchange: Foreign currency can be exchanged for Mauritian rupees at banks, authorized money changers, and airport currency exchange counters. Banks generally provide competitive exchange rates, and it's a good idea to compare rates and fees before completing a transaction.

ATMs: ATMs are widely available in Mauritius' major cities and tourist areas. You can withdraw Mauritian rupees using your international debit or credit card. Although Visa and Mastercard are widely accepted, it is best to notify your bank before traveling to ensure that your cards will work properly abroad. Withdrawal limits may apply at some ATMs, so be aware of any restrictions.

Credit Cards: Credit cards, particularly Visa and Mastercard, are widely accepted in Mauritius' hotels, resorts, restaurants, and larger establishments. However, carrying cash is always a good idea for smaller businesses, local markets, and areas where card acceptance may be limited.

Traveler's Cheques: Traveler's cheques are not widely accepted in Mauritius, and finding places that will cash them can be difficult. It is advised to use alternative payment methods, such as debit or credit cards, or to carry enough cash.

Tipping is not required in Mauritius, but it is appreciated for good service. Some restaurants may include a service charge in the bill, which eliminates the need for an additional tip. If there is no service charge, it is customary to leave a 10% to 15% tip. Tipping hotel staff, taxi drivers, and tour guides is a personal preference based on the quality of service received.

Currency Restrictions: There are no specific limits on the amount of foreign currency that can be brought into Mauritius. However, if you have more than 500,000 Mauritian Rupees (approximately USD 12,500) in cash, you must declare it when you arrive.

It is advised to keep a reasonable amount of cash on hand for small expenses and emergencies. To avoid scams or counterfeit money, be cautious of your belongings and use reputable currency exchange services.

Because currency exchange rates fluctuate, it is best to check current rates and compare fees to ensure you get the best value for your money.

D. Getting to Mauritius

Because Mauritius is an island nation, most visitors arrive by plane. The following are the most common ways to get to Mauritius:

Flights: The main international gateway to Mauritius is Sir Seewoosagur Ramgoolam International Airport (MRU). Numerous airlines fly to and from major cities all over the world, including Europe, Asia, Africa, and the Middle East. There are direct flights to Mauritius from cities such as Paris, London, Johannesburg, Dubai, Singapore, and Mumbai, among others. Flight duration can vary depending on the origin and route.

Connecting Flights: If no direct flights are available from your location, you can book connecting flights to Mauritius via one of the major international airports. Several airlines provide connecting flights to Mauritius, providing travelers with convenient options.

Cruise Ships: While less common than air travel, some cruise ships visit Mauritius. Cruising to Mauritius provides a scenic journey, but check the itineraries and schedules of cruise lines that visit the island.

Immigration and customs procedures must be completed upon arrival in Mauritius. Make sure you have a valid passport with a validity period that extends beyond your planned stay. Visa requirements may differ depending on your nationality, so check the specific visa regulations and obtain the necessary documentation ahead of time, if applicable.

To secure the best fares and ensure a smooth journey to Mauritius, book your travel arrangements well in advance.

E. Transportation in Mauritius

Mauritius' transportation system is primarily made up of public and private modes of transportation. Here are some of the most common ways to get around in Mauritius:

Taxis: Taxis can be hailed on the street or found at designated taxi stands in Mauritius. They use a metered fare system, but it's best to confirm the fare before beginning your journey. Because some taxis do not have meters, it is best to negotiate the fare ahead of time. Taxis are a good choice for short trips or private transportation.

Buses: The Mauritius public bus network is extensive and reasonably priced. Most areas of the island are served by buses, including major towns, tourist attractions, and residential areas. The buses are color-coded by route, and schedules are available at bus stations or online. While buses are a cost-effective option, they can be crowded and schedules are not always strictly adhered to.

Car Rental: Renting a car is a popular option for visitors who want to explore Mauritius on their own. On the island, there are several car rental companies, and driving is done on the left side of the road. To rent and drive a car in Mauritius, you must have a valid international driving license or a local driving permit. Before driving, it is critical to become acquainted with the local traffic rules and road conditions.

Scooters and Motorcycles: Rentals of scooters and motorcycles are available in tourist areas. They provide a convenient and flexible way to navigate the island, especially in congested areas. Renting and riding a scooter or motorcycle, like renting a car, requires a valid international driving license or a local permit.

Trains: Mauritius has a limited train service that connects certain towns, primarily on the central plateau. While the train network is not extensive, it can be a scenic way to explore the interior of the island.

Bicycle Rental: For those who prefer a more environmentally friendly mode of transportation, bicycle rentals are available in some tourist areas. It enables leisurely exploration of the surroundings, particularly in coastal areas.

It is critical to plan your transportation ahead of time based on your itinerary and preferences. In remote areas, public transportation options may be limited, so check schedules and plan accordingly. Private transportation options, such as taxis or car rentals, offer greater flexibility for longer distances or specific destinations.

In urban areas, traffic congestion can occur during peak hours, so allow extra time for travel. It's also critical to have the right navigation tools, maps, or a GPS to help you get to your destination.

Finally, when using any mode of transportation in Mauritius, always prioritize your safety and follow local traffic rules and regulations.

F. Accommodation Options

Mauritius has a diverse range of accommodation options to suit a variety of tastes and budgets. The following are some of the most common types of accommodations on the island:

Hotels and Resorts: Mauritius has a diverse range of hotels and resorts that cater to a variety of preferences and budgets, ensuring a memorable stay for every visitor.

Grand Baie, located along the northern coast, is a popular area known for its hotel and resort offerings. With its beautiful beaches, lively atmosphere, and exciting water sports activities, Grand Baie offers a variety of lodging options, ranging from luxurious to more affordable.

Flic-en-Flac, on the west coast, enchants visitors with its long sandy beach and crystal-clear turquoise waters. This is an excellent location for sunbathing, snorkeling, and diving. Flic-en-Flac has a variety of hotels and resorts, including all-inclusive options, to ensure a relaxing and enjoyable stay.

Belle Mare, on the east coast, has beautiful beaches and luxurious resorts. This serene setting is ideal for those looking for a peaceful and upscale retreat. The resorts in Belle Mare provide world-class amenities, spa facilities, and even golf courses, allowing guests to relax and enjoy leisure activities.

Le Morne, located on Mauritius' southwestern tip, is home to the iconic Le Morne Brabant mountain and a picturesque lagoon. This area has a mix of luxury resorts and boutique hotels, creating an intimate and secluded atmosphere for an unforgettable vacation.

Mauritius hotels and resorts provide a variety of amenities and services to enhance guests' comfort and enjoyment. Common amenities include spacious rooms or suites, on-site restaurants and bars, swimming pools, fitness centers, and spa facilities. Water sports activities, kids' clubs, and entertainment options are also available at some establishments, ensuring that there is something for everyone.

When choosing a hotel or resort in Mauritius, consider factors like location, amenities, reviews, and budget. Given the popularity of these accommodations, it is best to book ahead of time, especially during peak travel seasons, to ensure your preferred choice and dates for your stay in Mauritius.

Guesthouses and Bed and Breakfasts: Mauritius has a wide range of guesthouses and bed and breakfasts that offer travelers a charming and personalized accommodation experience. These establishments can be found throughout the island, each with its own distinct charm and ambiance.

Guesthouses and bed and breakfasts can be found in the city center or nearby neighborhoods of Port Louis, the capital city. This allows visitors to discover the cultural attractions, markets, and museums that define the character of the capital.

Heading south, Mahebourg welcomes visitors with its historical significance and proximity to the international airport. Guesthouses and bed and breakfasts provide a comfortable stay near the town's colonial architecture, waterfront promenade, and nature reserves.

Trou d'Eau Douce, on the east coast, entices visitors with its idyllic fishing village atmosphere. This area's guesthouses and bed and breakfasts provide a relaxed and intimate setting for guests to enjoy the stunning beaches, boat trips to Île aux Cerfs, and water sports activities.

Chamarel, in the southwest, reveals its natural wonders, including the well-known Seven Colored Earths and Chamarel Waterfall. Guesthouses and bed and breakfasts provide a cozy haven for nature lovers, allowing them to explore the unique landscapes and hiking trails.

Tamarin, on the western coast, is a popular destination for surfers, dolphin watchers, and sunset enthusiasts. Guesthouses and bed and breakfasts in this area provide a relaxing beachside experience with easy access to water activities and nearby attractions.

Mauritius' guesthouses and bed and breakfasts take pride in their warm hospitality and personalized service. Guests can expect comfortable rooms or suites, communal areas for socializing, and delectable home-cooked breakfasts featuring island flavors.

It is recommended that when choosing a guesthouse or bed and breakfast in Mauritius, you conduct extensive research on the amenities, location, and reviews to find an establishment that matches your preferences. Due to the popularity of these accommodations, it's best to book ahead of time, especially during peak travel seasons, to ensure you get your preferred choice and dates for your stay in Mauritius.

Villas and Vacation Rentals: Mauritius has a fantastic selection of villas and vacation rentals, making it an ideal choice for those looking for privacy, space, and a home-away-from-home experience.

These accommodations are designed to provide plenty of space, making them ideal for families, groups, or couples seeking privacy and independence. Multiple bedrooms, living areas, fully equipped kitchens, private gardens, and swimming pools are common features of villas and vacation rentals, allowing guests to relax and unwind in their own private space.

Villas and vacation rentals, with a focus on comfort and convenience, offer modern amenities such as comfortable beds, well-equipped kitchens, entertainment systems, and outdoor lounging areas. They are intended to create a homey atmosphere that will make guests feel at ease during their stay.

One of the benefits of villas and vacation rentals is the freedom and flexibility they provide. Guests can plan their own schedules, prepare their own meals, and have a more personalized vacation experience. There are no restrictions on dining hours or other hotel policies, giving guests a sense of independence.

Many Mauritius villas and vacation rentals are strategically located in picturesque settings, such as along the coastline, overlooking the ocean, or nestled in lush tropical gardens. These locations offer breathtaking views and a tranquil environment, allowing guests to immerse themselves in the island's natural beauty.

These accommodations are ideal for larger groups or families traveling together. They provide shared spaces for socializing and spending quality time together, as well as private bedrooms for privacy and relaxation.

When looking for a Mauritius villa or vacation rental, check the amenities, location, and reviews to ensure it meets your specific needs and preferences. To secure your preferred choice and dates for your stay in Mauritius, book in advance, especially during peak travel seasons.

Self-Catering Apartments: Self-catering apartments in Mauritius offer a convenient and flexible lodging option for travelers who prefer independence and the ability to prepare their own meals.

These apartments allow guests to create their own schedules and enjoy a more flexible vacation experience. You can prepare meals according to your preferences and dietary needs with a fully equipped kitchen. This freedom allows you to dine whenever you want, without regard to hotel restaurant hours.

Self-catering apartments can also be a good value, especially for longer stays or larger groups. Cooking your own meals allows you to save money on dining out and have more control over your budget. Grocery shopping and exploring local markets can also result in an immersive culinary experience.

These apartments provide a private and comfortable environment, much like being at home. You can relax and unwind in your own space, creating a sense of privacy and comfort, with separate living areas, bedrooms, bathrooms, and a fully furnished kitchen.

Self-catering apartments include essential amenities such as kitchen appliances, cookware, utensils, and dining areas to make your stay more comfortable. They may also provide extra services such as Wi-Fi, laundry facilities, and access to communal areas such as swimming pools or gardens.

Self-catering apartments can be found throughout Mauritius, including popular tourist destinations like Grand Baie, Flic-en-Flac, Trou aux Biches, and Belle Mare. Accommodation options in these areas include apartments within residential complexes and standalone villas with self-catering facilities.

When looking for a self-catering apartment in Mauritius, it's a good idea to look into the amenities, location, and reviews to make sure it meets your needs. To secure your preferred choice and dates for your stay in Mauritius, book in advance, especially during peak travel seasons.

Eco-Lodges and Nature Retreats: The island of Mauritius is home to enchanting eco-lodges and nature retreats that allow visitors to immerse themselves in the island's natural beauty while minimizing their environmental impact.

These eco-lodges and nature retreats are often located in peaceful and scenic settings, surrounded by lush forests, pristine beaches, or verdant mountains. They provide a distinct blend of comfort, sustainability, and a strong connection to nature.

These eco-lodges and nature retreats can be found throughout Mauritius. Some popular spots include:

Chamarel: Chamarel, located in southwest Mauritius, is known for its stunning landscapes, including the iconic Seven Colored Earths and Chamarel Waterfall. The area has eco-lodges that blend in with the natural surroundings, offering guests a peaceful retreat.

Black River Gorges National Park: Located in the island's southwest, the Black River Gorges National Park is a nature lover's paradise. It has a wide variety of flora and fauna, hiking trails, and panoramic views. Eco-lodges near the park provide easy access to the park's wonders.

Rodrigues Island: Rodrigues Island, a smaller island in the Mascarene archipelago, is known for its untouched natural beauty. Eco-lodges on the island offer a tranquil escape with opportunities for snorkeling, diving, and exploring the island's diverse ecosystems.

Bel Ombre: Located on Mauritius' southern coast, Bel Ombre is known for its pristine beaches and abundance of wildlife. Eco-lodges in this area provide a peaceful setting with opportunities to explore nearby nature reserves and participate in activities such as birdwatching and hiking.

These eco-lodges and nature retreats are built with sustainability in mind. Solar power, water conservation, organic gardens, and eco-friendly materials are among the environmentally friendly features they incorporate. Guests can enjoy eco-friendly amenities while being surrounded by Mauritius' natural wonders.

When looking for an eco-lodge or nature retreat in Mauritius, it's a good idea to look into the unique features and initiatives of each establishment. Look for certifications or affiliations with well-known environmental organizations. To secure your preferred choice and dates for your stay in Mauritius, book in advance, especially during peak travel seasons.

To secure the best options and rates, it is recommended that you book your accommodation in advance, especially during peak travel seasons. Many Mauritius accommodations can be booked online via various travel websites or directly through the property's official website. When deciding on the best type of accommodation for your needs, keep your preferences, budget, and desired location in mind.

Chapter 2: Top Tourist Destinations

A. Port Louis

Port Louis, Mauritius' capital city, is a vibrant and bustling destination that highlights the country's rich history, cultural diversity, and lively atmosphere. Port Louis, located on the northwest coast, provides visitors with a diverse range of attractions and experiences.

The Champs de Mars racecourse, the oldest horse racing track in the Southern Hemisphere, is a prominent landmark in Port Louis. The racecourse is important in Mauritian culture, and attending a race event is an exciting experience.

Those looking to immerse themselves in local culture should pay a visit to the Central Market. Visitors can peruse the various stalls selling fresh produce, spices, handicrafts, and souvenirs. The market is a hive of activity that offers a glimpse into Mauritius' daily life and trading traditions.

Caudan Waterfront is another popular destination in Port Louis, with a variety of shopping, dining, and entertainment options. This waterfront complex includes boutiques, restaurants, cafes, and a casino. It's a great place to unwind, enjoy a meal with a view, or do some retail therapy.

The Blue Penny Museum is a fascinating attraction for those interested in history and culture. It houses an impressive collection of artifacts and exhibits depicting Mauritius' history, art, and cultural heritage. The display of the famous Blue Penny and Red Penny stamps, considered among the rarest and most valuable stamps in the world, is one of the highlights.

Aapravasi Ghat, a UNESCO World Heritage site, is significant historically. During the nineteenth and early twentieth centuries, it served as an immigration depot for indentured laborers arriving from India, Africa, and other parts of the world. Visitors can explore the site and learn about the laborers' stories and struggles, which helped shape the island's multicultural identity.

Port Louis has a mix of modern and colonial architecture, with buildings like the Government House and the Municipal Theater highlighting the city's architectural heritage. The city's charm and appeal are enhanced by its vibrant street life, diverse cuisine, and colorful festivals.

Exploring Port Louis allows you to see the heart and soul of Mauritius. A visit to Port Louis promises a memorable experience for every traveler, whether it's discovering historical landmarks, indulging in local cuisine, or soaking up the lively atmosphere.

B. Grand Baie

Grand Baie is a popular tourist destination on Mauritius' northern coast. Grand Baie, known for its picturesque beaches, crystal-clear waters, and lively atmosphere, has a variety of attractions and activities for visitors to enjoy.

Grand Baie's main draw is its beautiful beaches. The golden sands and turquoise waters are ideal for sunbathing, swimming, and water sports. Pereybere Beach, in particular, is a popular destination for both locals and tourists, thanks to its calm waters and vibrant beach scene.

Water sports enthusiasts will be spoiled for choice in Grand Baie. Snorkeling, diving, sailing, and deep-sea fishing are popular activities in the area. Catamaran cruises are a popular option for visitors who want to explore nearby islands, take in breathtaking views, and even swim with dolphins.

Grand Baie is known for its vibrant nightlife in addition to its natural beauty. After sunset, the town comes alive, with numerous bars, clubs, and restaurants offering live music, DJ sets, and a wide range of cuisines. Its lively atmosphere makes it a popular destination for those looking for entertainment and a taste of the local nightlife.

The variety of shops, boutiques, and markets in Grand Baie will delight shoppers. The Grand Baie Bazaar is a bustling market where visitors can browse a variety of goods such as clothing, accessories, souvenirs, and local handicrafts. Another popular destination is the La Croisette shopping mall, which has a variety of international brands, restaurants, and a cinema.

The SSR Botanic Garden is nearby for those looking for a break from the beach and shopping. This vast garden is home to a diverse collection of plants, both indigenous and exotic. Visitors can enjoy leisurely walks through the park, admire the beautiful flora, and even spot giant water lilies in the pond.

Grand Baie offers the ideal combination of relaxation, entertainment, and natural beauty. Whether you want to relax on the beach, explore the underwater world, participate in thrilling water sports, shop and dine, or enjoy the vibrant nightlife, Grand Baie has something for everyone.

C. Black River Gorges National Park

The Black River Gorges National Park is a magnificent nature reserve in Mauritius' southwest. It is the largest national park on the island, covering over 67 square kilometers, and is a haven for nature lovers and outdoor enthusiasts.

The park's lush greenery, rugged terrain, and diverse ecosystems distinguish it. It is an important conservation area because it is home to several rare and endemic plant and animal species. The park's primary goal is to protect the island's native forests and provide a haven for the island's unique biodiversity.

The network of hiking trails in Black River Gorges National Park is one of its highlights. These trails wind through dense forests, providing stunning views, cascading waterfalls, and panoramic vistas. The trails cater to various fitness levels, ranging from easy walks to more difficult hikes. Maccabees Trail, Black River Peak Trail, and Alexandra Falls Viewpoint Trail are among the most popular.

With over 150 bird species recorded, the park is also a birdwatcher's paradise. Colorful endemic birds such as the Mauritius kestrel, pink pigeon, and echo parakeet can be seen by visitors. Within the park, the Ebony Forest Reserve is an excellent spot for birdwatching and discovering rare plant species, including the iconic ebony trees.

The park is dotted with scenic viewpoints that provide breathtaking views of the surrounding landscapes. These viewpoints allow visitors to take in the park's natural beauty, from the dramatic gorges and valleys to the distant mountains and coastline.

The Black River Gorges National Park is both a natural and educational destination. The park has interpretation centers and information boards that provide information about the park's flora and fauna as well as conservation efforts. Visitors can learn about Mauritius' unique ecosystems as well as ongoing initiatives to protect and preserve the island's natural heritage.

Black River Gorges National Park offers a captivating experience for nature enthusiasts, whether it's hiking through pristine forests, observing endemic bird species, marveling at stunning waterfalls, or simply immersing oneself in the tranquility of nature. It's a place to connect with the island's natural heritage and appreciate the beauty and significance of its diverse ecosystems.

D. Chamarel Colored Earths

The Chamarel Colored Earths are a natural phenomenon and one of Mauritius' most iconic attractions. This geological wonder is located in the village of Chamarel, in the southwestern part of the island, and consists of sand dunes with vivid and distinct colors, creating a mesmerizing sight.

The Chamarel Colored Earths are truly remarkable because of the color variation displayed by the dunes. The sand varies in color from red, brown, and violet to blue and green, resulting in a surreal and picturesque landscape. The colors are caused by weathering of volcanic rock, which has resulted in the formation of various mineral compounds in the sand.

The Chamarel Colored Earths can be explored by walking along designated pathways that provide a closer look at the dunes. The dunes are naturally layered, with the colors remaining distinct and distinct. It's a one-of-a-kind sight to see and a fantastic photo opportunity.

Visitors can admire the colored dunes while also visiting the nearby Chamarel Waterfall. This breathtaking waterfall cascades from a height of about 100 meters into a lush green gorge, creating an unforgettable backdrop. The site has viewing platforms where visitors can take in the beauty of the waterfall and surrounding landscapes.

There are facilities and attractions nearby that complement the Chamarel Colored Earths experience. The Seven Colored Earths Geopark teaches visitors about the geological processes that caused the phenomenon. It provides interpretive displays, information boards, and guided tours that delve into the site's scientific aspects.

Visitors can also visit the nearby Chamarel Rhumerie, a rum distillery. You can learn about the rum-making process, sample different rum flavors, and even buy bottles as souvenirs. The distillery is surrounded by lovely sugarcane fields, which adds to the allure of the visit.

The Chamarel Colored Earths is a must-see attraction for Mauritius visitors. The surreal and vibrant colors of the dunes, combined with the picturesque waterfall and the chance to learn about geological processes, make it a one-of-a-kind and unforgettable experience. It is a testament to the natural wonders found on the island and showcases Mauritius' beauty and diversity.

E. Pamplemousses Botanical Garden

Pamplemousses Botanical Garden, also known as Sir Seewoosagur Ramgoolam Botanical Garden, is one of the Southern Hemisphere's oldest and most renowned botanical gardens. The garden, which is located in the village of Pamplemousses in the northern part of Mauritius, is a haven of natural beauty and botanical wonders.

Pamplemousses Botanical Garden is home to an impressive collection of native and exotic plants and trees spread across a large area. The garden has a long history, dating back to the 18th century when it was founded by French horticulturist Pierre Poivre.

Pamplemousses Botanical Garden visitors can explore its well-kept pathways and discover a diverse range of plant species. Giant water lilies, towering palm trees, colorful tropical flowers, and fragrant spice trees are among the highlights. The garden is famous for its collection of rare and endemic plants, including the famous talipot palm, which flowers once and then dies.

The Victoria Amazonica water lilies are one of the garden's main attractions. These massive lily pads can grow to be three meters in diameter, creating an enthralling sight on the tranquil ponds. Visitors can get a close look at these magnificent water lilies and marvel at their size and beauty.

Visitors will come across charming features such as fountains, ponds, and gazebos as they stroll through the garden, adding to the peaceful ambiance. The scenic surroundings make it an ideal location for a leisurely walk, a picnic, or simply finding a quiet spot to relax in nature.

Pamplemousses Botanical Garden is also historically significant because it is home to the Château de Mon Plaisir. This elegant colonial mansion was once the residence of the French governor and is now a museum displaying antique colonial furniture and artifacts.

The garden is not only a delight for plant enthusiasts, but it is also a haven for birdwatchers. Several bird species, including the famous Mauritius kestrel, can be seen among the foliage, making it an ideal destination for nature enthusiasts.

A visit to Pamplemousses Botanical Garden is both relaxing and educational. It allows visitors to appreciate nature's beauty, learns about various plant species, and immerse themselves in Mauritius' rich botanical heritage. It is a place where history, culture, and natural beauty coexist to create a delightful oasis for all who enter its gates.

F. Trou aux Cerfs

Trou aux Cerfs is a dormant volcano in the center of Mauritius, near the town of Curepipe. It is one of the island's most visible and easily accessible volcanic craters. Because of its unique geological features and breathtaking views, this natural wonder attracts both locals and tourists.

The Trou aux Cerfs crater is approximately 85 meters deep and 350 meters in diameter, making it a breathtaking sight. It is distinguished by steep slopes covered in lush green vegetation, which creates a picturesque backdrop. The shape and formation of the crater provide visitors with an insight into the island's volcanic past.

The summit of Trou aux Cerfs can be reached by following a well-kept path that winds its way up the slopes. They are rewarded with panoramic views of the surrounding landscape once they reach the top. On a clear day, the entire town of Curepipe, as well as the distant mountains and even the coastline, can be seen.

Visitors can admire the beauty and diversity of Mauritius' topography from Trou aux Cerfs. The rolling hills, forests, sugarcane plantations, and residential areas that stretch out in every direction can be seen from the crater's rim. The ever-changing play of light and shadow across the landscape adds to the experience's allure.

Trou aux Cerfs has a serene and tranquil atmosphere in addition to its natural beauty. Joggers, walkers, and nature enthusiasts frequent the area surrounding the crater to enjoy the fresh air and peaceful surroundings. It's the ideal place to unwind and reconnect with nature.

Trou aux Cerfs offers a chance for those interested in science to learn about volcanism and Mauritius' geological history. Around the crater, information boards provide educational insights into the formation and significance of this natural wonder.

Visiting Trou aux Cerfs entails not only observing the volcanic crater but also immersing oneself in the natural beauty of the surroundings. It provides an opportunity to appreciate Mauritius' natural wonders and witness the incredible forces that shaped the island's landscape. Trou aux Cerfs promises a memorable experience for nature lovers and curious explorers alike, whether it's enjoying the panoramic views, taking a leisurely walk, or simply embracing the peaceful ambiance.

G. Le Morne Brabant

Le Morne Brabant is a stunning UNESCO World Heritage Site located on Mauritius's southwest coast. It is a stunning natural landmark formed by a dramatic mountain and peninsula rising majestically from the Indian Ocean.

Le Morne Brabant is historically and culturally significant. It was a haven for escaped slaves known as maroons during the 18th and 19th centuries. These brave souls sought refuge on the inaccessible mountain, establishing a distinct community with its own customs, traditions, and Creole language.

Le Morne Brabant is now a popular tourist destination, attracting visitors with its stunning natural beauty and rich history. The rugged cliffs, lush vegetation, and pristine beaches that surround the mountain's base make it famous.

Many daring visitors attempt the difficult hike to the summit of Le Morne Brabant. The hike requires navigating steep slopes and rocky terrain, but the reward is well worth the effort. Hikers are greeted at the top with breathtaking panoramic views of the ocean, coastline, and Mauritius' lush landscapes. It's a truly unforgettable experience that highlights the island's natural beauty.

Le Morne Brabant is a place of remembrance and reflection, in addition to its natural beauty. A memorial to the maroons and the history of slavery in Mauritius can be found at the mountain's base. This serves as a poignant reminder of the island's history and the tenacity of those who fought for liberty.

Le Morne Brabant's surroundings provide opportunities for relaxation and recreation. With crystal-clear waters teeming with marine life, the pristine beaches are ideal for sunbathing, swimming, and snorkeling. Due to the consistent winds and favorable conditions, water sports such as kiteboarding and windsurfing are also popular in this region.

Le Morne Brabant is more than just a beautiful mountain; it is a synthesis of natural beauty, cultural heritage, and historical significance. Visitors can immerse themselves in the stunning landscapes, learn about the island's history, and admire the maroons' resilience. A visit to Le Morne Brabant is a memorable and enriching experience, whether hiking to the summit, relaxing on the beaches, or simply admiring the breathtaking views.

H. Ile aux Cerfs

Ile aux Cerfs, also known as Deer Island, is a beautiful paradise off Mauritius' east coast. This idyllic island is known for its pristine white sandy beaches, turquoise waters, and abundance of natural beauty.

The picturesque beaches of Ile aux Cerfs are the island's main draw. The island has powdery sands that are ideal for sunbathing, strolling along the beach, or simply relaxing under a palm tree. The island's crystal-clear waters are ideal for swimming and snorkeling, allowing visitors to explore the vibrant marine life and coral reefs.

The variety of water sports and recreational activities available on Ile aux Cerfs is one of its highlights. Visitors can enjoy thrilling activities like parasailing, water skiing, jet skiing, and windsurfing. Boat trips and catamaran cruises are also popular, giving visitors the opportunity to explore the surrounding lagoons, visit nearby islands, and spend a relaxing day on the water.

There are secluded coves and peaceful spots on the island where one can simply relax and enjoy the serenity of nature for those seeking tranquility. Ile aux Cerfs provides an escape from the hustle and bustle of daily life, allowing visitors to unwind and reconnect with the natural beauty of their surroundings.

Ile aux Cerfs has a championship golf course in addition to its natural attractions. The world-famous Ile aux Cerfs Golf Club, designed by professional golfer Bernhard Langer, provides a world-class golfing experience in a breathtaking tropical setting. Golfers can tee off against a backdrop of stunning ocean views and lush landscapes.

Restaurants and beach bars are available on the island for visitors to enjoy delicious local cuisine and refreshing tropical beverages. The relaxed atmosphere, combined with the breathtaking scenery, makes for an unforgettable dining experience.

Visitors can take a boat transfer from various departure points along Mauritius' east coast to Ile aux Cerfs. The journey itself is frequently enjoyable, with scenic views of the coastline and the chance to see dolphins swimming in the open sea.

Ile aux Cerfs is a slice of paradise that enchants visitors with its natural beauty, beautiful beaches, and a variety of activities. A visit to Ile aux Cerfs guarantees a memorable tropical island experience, whether it's engaging in thrilling water sports, relaxing on the pristine sands, or simply enjoying the scenic views.

Chapter 3: Experiencing Nature and Wildlife

A. Underwater Activities: Snorkeling and Diving

Because of its clear waters, vibrant coral reefs, and diverse marine life, underwater activities such as snorkeling and diving are extremely popular in Mauritius.

Snorkeling allows you to explore the underwater world without requiring any special training or equipment. Mauritius has several snorkeling spots that are easily accessible. Blue Bay Marine Park in the southeast is famous for its vibrant coral gardens and diverse marine life. Trou aux Biches, in the northwest, has calm and shallow waters that are ideal for snorkeling. Flic-en-Flac on the west coast is known for its vibrant marine ecosystem, which includes a wide variety of fish and coral formations.

Divers will find numerous opportunities to explore the depths of Mauritius' waters. Coin de Mire, located in the island's northernmost region, provides thrilling diving opportunities. The dive sites surrounding this beautiful islet offer spectacular coral formations, underwater caves, and encounters with marine creatures such as moray eels, lionfish, and reef sharks.

Cathedral, a cavern dive near Flic-en-Flac with beautiful rock formations, and Roche Zozo, known for its underwater arches and swim-throughs, are two other popular dive sites. The wrecks of Stella Maru and Djabeda offer exciting diving opportunities for both novice and experienced divers.

Divers in Mauritius can expect to see a diverse range of marine life, including colorful fish, sea turtles, rays, and even dolphins. Diving in Mauritius is a memorable experience due to the warm waters and excellent visibility.

Whether you prefer snorkeling or diving, Mauritius' underwater world promises an unforgettable adventure. Exploring the vibrant coral reefs and encountering marine creatures is an experience you won't want to miss, thanks to its diverse marine ecosystems and captivating scenery.

B. Dolphin and Whale Watching

Dolphin and whale watching is a popular activity in Mauritius, providing a once-in-a-lifetime opportunity to observe these magnificent marine creatures in their natural environment.

Mauritius is home to a variety of dolphin species, including spinner dolphins, bottlenose dolphins, and even rare and endangered humpback dolphins. These intelligent and playful creatures are frequently spotted in the waters surrounding the island, especially early in the morning.

Dolphin-watching excursions are typically available from coastal towns such as Tamarin, Flic-en-Flac, and Black River. The tours take you out to sea, where you can watch the dolphins perform acrobatics in the water alongside the boats. Some tours even allow visitors to swim with dolphins, making for an unforgettable experience.

Mauritius attracts migratory whale species in addition to dolphins at certain times of the year. Humpback and sperm whales are the most commonly seen species. As they navigate the ocean waters around the island, these majestic creatures can be seen breaching and spouting water.

The best time to go dolphin and whale watching in Mauritius is between May and November. During this time, the seas are generally calmer, and you have a better chance of seeing these marine mammals.

It is critical to select a responsible and eco-friendly tour operator who adheres to guidelines to ensure the well-being and conservation of marine animals. Respect for their natural environment is essential, and regulations like keeping a safe distance and avoiding any disturbance should be prioritized.

Dolphin and whale watching in Mauritius is an enthralling experience that allows you to get up close and personal with these incredible creatures while learning about their behavior and habitat. It's a once-in-a-lifetime chance to connect with nature and appreciate the beauty of the ocean's inhabitants in their natural habitat.

C. Casela Nature and Leisure Park

Casela Nature and Leisure Park is a popular attraction in Mauritius' western region. The park, which spans a large area, provides a unique blend of nature, adventure, and wildlife experiences for visitors of all ages.

Casela Nature Park's diverse wildlife is one of its main draws. Animals found in the park include zebras, giraffes, lions, tigers, monkeys, giant tortoises, and many others. Visitors can take safari tours within the park to get up close and personal with these animals while learning about their habitats and behaviors.

Casela has a variety of exciting activities for adventure seekers. Activities such as zip-lining, canyoning, quad biking, and Segway rides can provide an adrenaline rush. The park also has an aerial adventure course where you can navigate through high ropes, suspension bridges, and zip lines while taking in the scenery.

Casela Nature Park offers opportunities to immerse yourself in Mauritius' natural beauty in addition to wildlife and adventure. The scenic landscapes of the park, with lush vegetation, mountains, and cascading waterfalls, create a serene and tranquil atmosphere.

Children can enjoy the park's dedicated areas, such as the Petting Farm, where they can interact with friendly farm animals, or the Children's Playground, which offers a variety of fun activities.

Casela Nature Park is also committed to conservation and education. It runs several programs and initiatives to raise awareness about the importance of wildlife conservation and environmental preservation.

Visitors to Casela can take advantage of on-site amenities such as restaurants and picnic areas, allowing them to spend the entire day exploring and relaxing.

Casela Nature and Leisure Park, located near Flic-en-Flac and the Black River, is easily accessible from Mauritius' major tourist areas. It provides a well-rounded experience that combines wildlife encounters, adventure activities, and natural beauty, making it a popular destination for families, adventure seekers, and nature lovers.

D. La Vanille Nature Park

La Vanille Nature Park is a one-of-a-kind attraction in Mauritius' south. It is a sanctuary for various animal species, particularly reptiles, and allows visitors to learn about and interact with these fascinating creatures.

The impressive collection of crocodiles at La Vanille Nature Park is one of the park's main draws. The park has thousands of Nile crocodiles, making it one of the world's largest crocodile reserves. Visitors can get up close and personal with these ancient reptiles, as well as witness crocodile feedings, which are both thrilling and educational.

Aside from crocodiles, La Vanille Nature Park is home to a variety of other reptiles, including giant tortoises, iguanas, geckos, and chameleons. The park's Tortoise Park is especially noteworthy because it provides a home for these magnificent creatures, some of which are over a century old.

In addition to reptiles, the park has a mini-farm where visitors can interact with farm animals like goats, rabbits, and deer. There's also a butterfly garden where you can see a colorful variety of butterfly species fluttering around in a natural tropical setting.

The emphasis at La Vanille Nature Park is on education and conservation. It provides guided tours and educational displays about the biology, behavior, and conservation efforts of the park's reptiles and other animals.

For those looking for a one-of-a-kind experience, the park allows visitors to hold and photograph baby crocodiles and giant tortoises under the supervision of experienced handlers.

La Vanille Nature Park also has beautifully landscaped gardens with lush vegetation and exotic plants, in addition to animal exhibits. On-site picnic areas and a restaurant allow visitors to unwind and enjoy the natural surroundings.

La Vanille Nature Park is a place where visitors can learn about the fascinating world of reptiles, appreciate Mauritius' wildlife diversity, and learn about conservation efforts. It provides visitors of all ages with an interactive and educational experience that is both entertaining and informative.

E. Bird Watching in Ile aux Aigrettes

Ile aux Aigrettes is a small island nature reserve off Mauritius's southeastern coast. It is well-known for its diverse biodiversity, particularly as a haven for rare bird species. Birdwatchers will find Ile aux Aigrettes to be a haven for viewing rare avian life.

The opportunity to see the critically endangered Mauritius kestrel is one of the island's main draws for birdwatchers. Ile aux Aigrettes has been instrumental in the conservation of this bird, which was once on the verge of extinction. The Mauritius kestrel population has made a remarkable recovery as the island's ecosystem has been restored. Visitors to the island stand a good chance of seeing this magnificent raptor, which can be seen soaring through the sky or perched on the treetops.

Ile aux Aigrettes is home to a variety of endemic and migratory bird species, in addition to the

Mauritius Kestrel. The pink pigeon, a vibrant and rare bird found only in Mauritius, may be encountered. The endemic Mauritius Fody, a small songbird with distinctive red plumage, also nests on the island. The Mauritius Bulbul, Mascarene Paradise Flycatcher, and endangered Mauritius Olive White-eye are among the other bird species that can be seen.

On Ile aux Aigrettes, guided tours are available to enhance the birdwatching experience. Knowledgeable guides share information about the unique adaptations and behaviors of the birds you encounter, providing valuable insights into the island's avian biodiversity. They can also point out specific bird habitats and nesting areas, increasing your chances of seeing these enthralling creatures.

Birdwatchers should bring binoculars, cameras, and comfortable walking shoes when visiting Ile aux Aigrettes. Exploring the trails of the island and watching birds in their natural habitat is a truly rewarding experience. Ile aux Aigrettes' peaceful and untouched environment allows for uninterrupted birdwatching, making it a must-see destination for both bird enthusiasts and nature lovers.

It is important to note that access to Ile aux Aigrettes is restricted, and visits must be arranged through the Mauritian Wildlife Foundation. This protects the island's fragile ecosystem and ensures a long-term approach to birdwatching and conservation efforts.

F. Sir Seewoosagur Ramgoolam Botanical Garden

The Sir Seewoosagur Ramgoolam Botanical Garden, also known as the Pamplemousses Botanical Garden, is a well-known attraction in Mauritius' Pamplemousses district. It is one of the Southern Hemisphere's oldest botanical gardens and is known for its extensive collection of exotic plant species.

The botanical garden covers a large area, providing visitors with a tranquil and enchanting environment to explore. It is named after Sir Seewoosagur Ramgoolam, Mauritius' first Prime Minister, in recognition of his contributions to the country.

The garden contains an amazing variety of plant species, including towering palm trees, fragrant flowers, and exotic fruit trees. The garden's collection of giant water lilies, including the famous Victoria amazonica, is one of its main attractions. These magnificent lilies have large circular leaves that can withstand the weight of a small child and lovely white or pink flowers that bloom at night.

Visitors can stroll along the garden's well-kept pathways and discover a diverse collection of tropical plants and trees from all over the world. There are also several thematic sections in the garden, such as the spice garden, where you can learn about and see various spices used in traditional Mauritian cuisine.

There are tranquil ponds, cascading waterfalls, and charming gazebos throughout the garden that provide ideal spots for relaxation and appreciation of nature's beauty. It is a haven for nature lovers, photographers, and those looking for a peaceful escape from the hustle and bustle of city life.

The Sir Seewoosagur Ramgoolam Botanical Garden is home to a variety of bird species, including the Mauritius kestrel and the echo parakeet, in addition to its botanical wonders. Birdwatchers will have a great time spotting these vibrant avian residents as they explore the garden.

The botanical garden offers guided tours that provide valuable information about the various plant species, their medicinal uses, and their historical significance. The knowledgeable guides share fascinating anecdotes and information about the garden's rich heritage, as well as the critical role it plays in preserving Mauritius' natural treasures.

The Sir Seewoosagur Ramgoolam Botanical Garden, located near the capital city of Port Louis, is easily accessible to visitors from all over the island. It is a must-see for nature enthusiasts, botany enthusiasts, and anyone looking for a peaceful and captivating experience surrounded by the beauty of Mauritius' flora and fauna.

G. Rodrigues Island

Rodrigues Island is a small, picturesque island in the Indian Ocean about 560 kilometers (350 miles) east of Mauritius. It is a self-contained outer island of Mauritius that provides a tranquil and untouched retreat for visitors looking for a quieter and more laid-back experience.

Rodrigues Island is known for its breathtaking natural beauty, which includes pristine beaches, turquoise lagoons, and rugged terrain. The island's allure stems from its untouched and unspoiled environment, which offers a tranquil retreat away from the bustling tourist crowds.

Rodrigues' beautiful beaches are one of its main draws. Gravier, Trou d'Argent, and Saint François are some of the most popular beaches on the island, where visitors can relax on powdery white sands, swim in crystal-clear waters, and take in the natural beauty of the island. These beaches are also great for snorkeling and diving, allowing you to explore vibrant coral reefs and encounter a variety of marine life.

The interior of the island is characterized by rolling hills, valleys, and a diverse agricultural landscape. Hikes and nature walks can be taken to explore the island's scenic trails, discover hidden waterfalls, and take in panoramic views of the surrounding seascape. Mont Limon and Mont Fanal are popular viewpoints with stunning views of Rodrigues' landscapes.

Rodrigues Island is also known for its warm and welcoming locals. The Rodriguans have their own culture and way of life that is deeply rooted in their Creole heritage. Visitors can interact with the locals, learn about their traditions, and sample the island's authentic cuisine. Don't pass up the opportunity to sample traditional dishes such as octopus curry, salted fish, and coconut-based desserts.

The marine ecosystem on the island is diverse and offers unique opportunities for ecotourism. Visitors can explore the Rodrigues Marine Reserve, a

2,000-hectare protected area teeming with marine life. Snorkeling, scuba diving, and boat trips are popular ways to see colorful coral reefs and tropical fish and even swim with dolphins and turtles.

Consider staying in one of Rodrigues' charming guesthouses or boutique hotels to truly experience the laid-back island lifestyle. These lodgings provide a more intimate and authentic experience and are frequently run by local families who can provide insights into the island's culture and traditions.

Rodrigues Island can be reached via regular flights from Mauritius. Visitors can get around the island by renting bicycles or scooters, hiring taxis, or using public transportation.

Rodrigues Island is a peaceful haven for those looking for natural beauty, cultural immersion, and a slower pace of life. Its pristine beaches, untouched landscapes, and warm hospitality make it a hidden gem within the Indian Ocean, ideal for a memorable and rejuvenating getaway.

Chapter 4: Beaches and Water Sports

A. Belle Mare Beach

Belle Mare Beach is a stunning stretch of coastline on Mauritius' east coast. It is well-known for its pristine beauty, calm waters, and powdery white sand, making it a popular beach and water sports destination.

The beach at Belle Mare provides a tranquil and picturesque setting ideal for relaxation and serenity. The azure blue waters lap gently against the shore, providing a relaxing setting for sunbathing, swimming, and beach walks. Visitors are invited to sink their toes into the soft, white sand and relax under the warm tropical sun.

Belle Mare Beach is both a relaxing haven and a playground for water sports enthusiasts. The calm and clear waters are ideal for a variety of activities. Windsurfing and kiteboarding are especially popular due to the area's consistent trade winds. As you glide over the waves or harness the power of the wind, the beach provides a sense of adventure.

For those looking for more adrenaline-pumping activities, Belle Mare Beach is a great place to go water skiing or jet skiing. Feel the rush of speed and exhilaration as you zoom across the water's surface. Another exciting option is parasailing, which allows you to soar above the beach and enjoy panoramic views of the coastline.

If you want to explore the vibrant underwater world, Belle Mare Beach has excellent snorkeling and diving opportunities. Grab your snorkel and mask for a breathtaking display of coral reefs teeming with vibrant tropical fish. Dive enthusiasts can go deeper into the ocean to see marine life like turtles, rays, and even reef sharks.

Along the coastline of Belle Mare Beach, there are several luxury resorts and hotels. These establishments provide beachfront lodging, allowing guests to wake up to the sound and sight of the ocean. Many resorts offer water sports facilities as well as equipment rentals, making it easy for guests to participate in their favorite activities.

Don't pass up the opportunity to see a breathtaking sunrise while visiting Belle Mare Beach. Mauritius' east coast is known for its spectacular sunrise views, and Belle Mare Beach is no exception. Early in the morning, watch the sun paint the sky with vibrant colors, casting a warm glow over the sparkling waters.

Whether you're looking for relaxation, adventure, or a little of both, Belle Mare Beach is a pristine tropical paradise that will satisfy your needs. With its natural beauty, calm waters, and abundance of water sports activities, it's no surprise that Belle Mare Beach is a favorite among Mauritius visitors.

B. Flic en Flac Beach

Flic-en-Flac Beach is a popular and vibrant coastal destination on Mauritius' west coast. It is famous for its beautiful stretches of sandy beach, clear waters, and lively atmosphere, which draws visitors from all over the world.

The beach at Flic-en-Flac is a long stretch of soft, golden sand that invites sunbathers to relax and enjoy the tropical atmosphere. The clear, turquoise waters lap gently against the shore, providing a peaceful setting for swimming and water activities. The beach is also lined with casuarina trees, which provide pockets of shade where you can escape the sun.

Water sports enthusiasts will love Flic-en-Flac Beach. The calm and warm waters provide ideal conditions for a variety of activities. Snorkeling and diving are popular activities due to the area's vibrant coral reefs and diverse marine life. Exploring the underwater world reveals a rainbow of colorful fish, fascinating coral formations, and even the possibility of encountering sea turtles.

Flic-en-Flac Beach offers water skiing, jet skiing, and parasailing for those looking for a little adventure. Feel an adrenaline rush as you zip across the water's surface, propelled by speed or the pull of a parachute. The beach is also a starting point for boat trips and catamaran cruises, which allow you to explore nearby islands, swim with dolphins, or simply enjoy the beauty of the coastline from a different angle.

Flic-en-Flac Beach is a popular destination not only during the day but also at night. There are numerous restaurants, bars, and beach clubs along the beach where you can enjoy delicious Mauritian cuisine, refreshing cocktails, and live music or entertainment. The vibrant nightlife adds to the area's excitement, creating a lively and festive atmosphere.

In addition to the beach, Flic-en-Flac has a variety of amenities and facilities to make your visit more enjoyable. Beachside vendors sell snacks, refreshments, and beach accessories. There are shops, supermarkets, and souvenir boutiques nearby where you can browse for local crafts and souvenirs.

Flic-en-Flac Beach is easily accessible, with plenty of parking for visitors arriving by car. It is also well-served by public transportation, making it a convenient destination for both locals and tourists. There are several hotels and resorts along or near the beach, offering accommodations ranging from luxury resorts to budget-friendly options.

Whether you want to soak up the rays, participate in water sports, or enjoy lively beachside entertainment, Flic-en-Flac Beach provides a vibrant and memorable experience. Its lovely surroundings, clear waters, and variety of activities make it a must-see for beachgoers and those looking for a fun-filled coastal getaway in Mauritius.

C. Tamarin Bay

Tamarin Bay is a picturesque coastal area on Mauritius' west coast. It is well-known for its beautiful beach, picturesque surroundings, and excellent surfing conditions, making it a popular tourist and local destination.

Tamarin Bay is known for its beautiful beach, which stretches along a crescent-shaped bay. The soft golden sand is ideal for sunbathing, lounging, and building sandcastles. The bay's crystal-clear waters provide a refreshing escape for swimming and cooling off in the tropical heat.

Tamarin Bay is especially popular with surfers because it has some of the best surfing conditions in Mauritius. The bay receives consistent swells from the Indian Ocean, resulting in consistent waves that attract surfers of all levels. The area is famous for its long left-hand reef break, which offers an exhilarating and challenging surfing experience. Beginners and those looking to learn or improve their skills can take advantage of surf schools and equipment rentals.

Tamarin Bay, in addition to surfing, provides other water sports activities. SUP (stand-up paddleboarding) is a popular activity that allows visitors to explore the bay's calm waters while getting a full-body workout. Another option is kayaking, which allows you to paddle along the coast and explore nearby coves and mangrove forests.

The presence of dolphins is one of Tamarin Bay's unique attractions. Dolphin-watching tours, which allow visitors to observe these graceful creatures in their natural habitat, are a popular activity in the area. The tours are typically held early in the morning when the dolphins are most active. Witnessing their playful behavior and possibly swimming alongside them in the open sea is an incredible experience.

The coastal area surrounding Tamarin Bay has beautiful scenery and exploration opportunities. The nearby Tamarin River estuary is a tranquil spot where visitors can take boat trips or stroll along its banks. The surrounding hills and mountains provide a beautiful backdrop for hiking and nature walks.

Tamarin Village, located near the bay, provides visitors with a variety of amenities and services. There are numerous restaurants, cafes, and beachfront bars where you can enjoy a meal or a refreshing drink while admiring the stunning ocean views. There are also grocery stores, shops, and lodging options ranging from guesthouses to luxury villas in the village.

Tamarin Bay is easily accessible by car, and there is parking available. There are also public transportation options, such as buses and taxis. Because of its convenient location, the bay is an excellent day trip destination from other parts of Mauritius.

Tamarin Bay offers a picturesque and vibrant coastal experience in Mauritius, whether you're a surfer looking for the perfect wave, a nature enthusiast seeking coastal beauty, or simply want to relax on a stunning beach.

D. Blue Bay Marine Park

Blue Bay Marine Park is a stunning marine protected area on Mauritius' southeast coast. It is well-known for its clear turquoise waters, vibrant coral reefs, and diverse marine life, making it a snorkeling and diving paradise.

The marine park covers approximately 353 hectares, including the lagoon and surrounding coral reefs. Blue Bay's pristine waters are teeming with a diverse range of marine species, making it a haven for underwater exploration. The park is home to over 50 coral species and over 70 fish species, including colorful tropical fish, reef sharks, rays, and even sea turtles.

Blue Bay Marine Park's stunning coral gardens are one of its highlights. The coral formations are a kaleidoscope of colors and shapes that create an amazing underwater landscape. Snorkelers can immerse themselves in this vibrant world by swimming among the corals and observing the diverse marine life that inhabits this ecosystem.

Diving is another popular activity in Blue Bay Marine Park, as it allows visitors to explore the reef's deeper layers. The marine park's dive sites cater to divers of all skill levels, from beginners to experienced enthusiasts. The dive sites offer a variety of underwater landscapes, such as coral walls, drop-offs, and swim-throughs, making for an enthralling diving experience.

Fishing is prohibited within the marine park boundaries to protect the marine ecosystem. This conservation effort has allowed marine life to flourish, creating a safe haven for a wide range of species. As a visitor to Blue Bay Marine Park, you must follow the rules and guidelines in place to protect this delicate ecosystem.

Blue Bay Marine Park can be reached by boat, with several operators offering snorkeling and diving excursions. These tours frequently include snorkeling equipment, expert guidance, and the opportunity to visit multiple snorkeling sites within the marine park.

Visitors to Blue Bay Marine Park can enjoy water activities such as glass-bottom boat tours and kayaking in addition to snorkeling and diving. Glass-bottom boat tours offer an unusual view of the underwater world, allowing you to observe marine life without getting wet. Kayaking allows you to explore the tranquil lagoon and its surroundings at your leisure.

Blue Bay Marine Park is easily accessible by car, with nearby parking available. It is also well-served by public transportation, making it easy for visitors to access the park.

If you enjoy nature or diving, a visit to Blue Bay Marine Park is a must-do while in Mauritius. Its pristine waters, vibrant coral reefs, and abundant marine life provide snorkelers, divers, and anyone looking to connect with the natural wonders of the ocean with an unforgettable experience.

E. Le Morne Beach

Le Morne Beach is a stunning coastal destination on Mauritius's southwest coast. It is famous for its untouched beauty, dramatic landscapes, and breathtaking views of the iconic Le Morne Brabant mountain.

With its fine, golden sand and crystal-clear turquoise waters, the beach at Le Morne provides a picturesque setting. It stretches for several kilometers, giving beachgoers plenty of space to relax, sunbathe, and enjoy the peaceful atmosphere. Swimming and water activities are ideal due to the gentle waves and calm waters.

Le Morne Beach is set against the backdrop of Le Morne Brabant, a UNESCO World Heritage site and a well-known Mauritius landmark. This majestic mountain rises majestically above the beach, creating a dramatic and breathtaking sight. The combination of the mountain, lush vegetation, and sparkling ocean creates a breathtaking natural landscape ideal for photography and exploration.

The beach at Le Morne is not only visually appealing, but it also provides ideal conditions for water sports. Kitesurfing and windsurfing are particularly popular in this region. The consistent trade winds and the large lagoon make these thrilling water sports possible. Kiteboarding schools and equipment rental services are available for both beginners and experienced riders.

Aside from water sports, Le Morne Beach is ideal for nature walks and hikes. The area around Le

Morne Brabant has several trails that lead to the mountain's summit. While the hike is difficult, you will be rewarded with panoramic views of the surrounding coastline, lagoon, and the vast Indian Ocean.

Le Morne Beach is also historically significant. During the 18th and 19th centuries, it served as a haven for runaway slaves. The mountain served as a natural fortress and hiding place for these fugitives, and it is now a symbol of resistance and the fight against slavery.

Visitors to Le Morne Beach will find a variety of nearby accommodations, ranging from luxury resorts to guesthouses, allowing them to stay close to this captivating coastal paradise. There are also restaurants and beachfront bars where you can savor delectable Mauritian cuisine while taking in panoramic ocean views.

Le Morne Beach is easily accessible by car, and parking facilities are available for visitors. Visitors can also take advantage of public transportation options such as buses and taxis.

Le Morne Beach offers a captivating destination that will leave you with lasting memories, whether you're looking for a relaxing beach experience, thrilling water sports, or an opportunity to explore the natural beauty and history of Mauritius.

F. Ile aux Benitiers

Ile aux Benitiers, also known as Benitiers Island, is a small and pristine island off Mauritius's southwest coast. It is a popular day trip destination that provides a tranquil and idyllic setting for those looking for a peaceful escape and a glimpse of untouched natural beauty.

The island is known for its pristine white sandy beaches, turquoise waters, and abundant marine life. It is surrounded by a coral reef, making it an ideal location for snorkeling and diving. The underwater world around Ile aux Benitiers is teeming with colorful fish, vibrant corals, and other fascinating marine species, making for an enthralling underwater exploration experience.

Ile aux Benitiers' serene and unspoiled beaches are one of its main draws. The island has secluded areas where visitors can relax, soak up the sun, and enjoy the peace and quiet. The shallow and calm waters surrounding the island are ideal for swimming and wading, providing a cool respite from the heat.

Aside from beach activities, Ile aux Benitiers is well-known for its fresh seafood. A delicious seafood barbecue prepared by local guides or boat operators is included in many day trips to the island. You can eat grilled fish, prawns, and other seafood delicacies while admiring the scenery and the gentle sea breeze.

In addition, the island is a popular starting point for excursions to the nearby underwater waterfall phenomenon. Even though it is an optical illusion caused by sand and currents, the sight of water cascading down from the ocean floor is truly mesmerizing and provides a one-of-a-kind photo opportunity.

Ile aux Benitiers is typically accessed by boat, and several tour operators and boat services offer day trips to the island. These tours frequently include transportation, snorkeling equipment, lunch, and the opportunity to visit other nearby attractions, such as dolphins in the surrounding waters.

It is recommended that you bring sunscreen, a hat, and drinking water when visiting Ile aux Benitiers. Because the island is primarily a day trip destination, there are no permanent accommodations. However, there are numerous lodging options on the mainland in areas such as Le Morne and Black River, from which you can easily access the island.

The unspoiled beauty of a secluded island paradise in Mauritius can be experienced by visiting Ile aux Benitiers. Its pristine beaches, clear waters, and abundant marine life provide a tranquil and memorable escape from the stresses of everyday life.

Chapter 5: Cultural Experiences and Festivals

A. Traditional Mauritian Cuisine

Mauritian cuisine is a delectable fusion of flavors and culinary influences from various cultures, including Indian, Creole, Chinese, and European. The dishes reflect the island's diverse heritage, creating a gastronomic experience rich in spices, aromatic herbs, and a delightful blend of sweet and savory flavors. Here are some traditional Mauritius dishes to try:

Dholl Puri: A type of flatbread made from ground split peas, Dholl Puri is a popular street food. It comes with a variety of fillings, such as curries, pickles, chutneys, and vegetables. Dholl puri is a must-try dish that exemplifies Mauritian cuisine's Indian influence.

Mauritian curries are known for their robust flavors and aromatic spices, such as chicken or fish curry. Chicken or fish is cooked in a fragrant sauce of cumin, coriander, turmeric, and ginger, as well as tomatoes, onions, and garlic. The result is a flavorful and satisfying curry that is frequently served with rice or roti.

Rougaille is a traditional Creole dish made with tomatoes, onions, garlic, and a mixture of spices. It can be made with a variety of ingredients, including chicken, fish, sausages, or tofu. Rougaille exemplifies Mauritian Creole cuisine and is frequently served with rice or bread.

Mine Frites: This Chinese-inspired dish combines noodles (typically egg noodles) with stir-fried vegetables, meat, or seafood. It's seasoned with soy sauce and other spices to make a savory and filling meal. Mine frites is a popular street food that can be found in a variety of local eateries.

Gateau Piment, also known as chili bites, is a popular snack in Mauritius. It is made up of deep-fried lentil fritters that have been seasoned with spices and chilies. Gateau Piment is crisp on the outside and soft on the inside, and it is typically served with chutney or sauce.

Farata: Farata is a type of flatbread from India, similar to roti. It's typically made of wheat flour and served with a variety of curries or as a wrap with fillings like bean curry, pickles, and chutneys. Farata is a Mauritian staple that can be eaten for breakfast, lunch, or dinner.

Pineapple and Mango Salad: With so many tropical fruits available in Mauritius, fruit salads are a refreshing and popular option. As a light and refreshing snack or dessert, a combination of ripe pineapple, mango, and other seasonal fruits is commonly prepared and enjoyed.

These are just a few of the varied and flavorful dishes that comprise traditional Mauritian cuisine. Exploring the local markets, street food stalls, and restaurants in Mauritius will provide ample opportunities to indulge in the island's delectable flavors and culinary delights.

B. Local Markets and Street Food

Mauritius is known for its vibrant local markets and delectable street food, which allow visitors to experience the island's authentic flavors and cultural diversity. Here are some notable local markets and popular street food options in Mauritius:

Local Markets:

Port Louis Central Market: Located in the capital city of Port Louis, this bustling market is a hive of activity. It sells a wide range of fresh fruits, vegetables, spices, and local products. There are also handicrafts, textiles, and souvenirs. Don't pass up the opportunity to try the street food stalls that serve traditional Mauritian snacks.

Flacq Market: The Flacq Market, located in the village of Flacq, is one of Mauritius' largest outdoor markets. It sells fresh produce, clothing, textiles, and local handicrafts. The market is particularly well-known for its selection of spices and traditional herbal remedies.

Quatre Bornes Market: Quatre Bornes Market is a popular shopping destination in the town of Quatre Bornes. It is well-known for its clothing, textiles, and accessories. There are also food stalls selling local delicacies, snacks, and refreshing drinks.

Street Food:

Dholl Puri: Dholl Puri is a must-try street food in Mauritius. It is a thin flatbread filled with a delicious blend of ground split peas and served with a variety of chutneys, pickles, and curries. Dholl Puri vendors can be found in many towns and cities, especially around lunchtime.

Roti Chaud: Roti Chaud is another popular street food. It is a soft, fluffy flatbread that is served with a variety of fillings, such as curry, chutney, pickles, and vegetables. Roti Chaud vendors can be found in a variety of locations, particularly in busy markets and towns.

Gateau Piment, also known as chili bites, are spicy lentil fritters that make for a flavorful and crispy snack. They are available at street food stalls and local markets. They are frequently served with tangy tamarind chutney.

Samosas are savory pastries filled with spiced vegetables, meat, or seafood. They're perfectly deep-fried and make a tasty snack. Samosas are commonly served with chutneys or sauces at many street food stalls.

Boulettes are dumplings filled with either meat or vegetables. They are usually served in a flavorful broth or with a tangy sauce. Boulettes can be found in specialized street food stalls or food courts.

Exploring local markets and trying street food in Mauritius is a delightful way to experience the island's authentic flavors and culinary traditions. These vibrant markets and mouthwatering street food options provide a true taste of the local culture and an opportunity to indulge in Mauritius' diverse and delicious cuisine.

C. Sega Dance and Music

Sega is a lively and rhythmic dance and music genre with deep cultural roots in Mauritius. It evolved from African slaves brought to the island during the colonial era. Sega is now a popular form of cultural expression and entertainment in Mauritius. Here's a peek into the enchantment that is Sega dance and music:

Sega's origins and influences can be traced back to the African rhythms and melodies brought to Mauritius by slaves. It gradually incorporated elements from Indian and European musical traditions, resulting in a distinctive fusion of styles. The lyrics of Sega's songs frequently reflect the Mauritian people's joys, sorrows, and daily struggles.

Musical Instruments: The ravanne (a large tambourine-like drum made of goat skin), the maravanne (a flat percussion instrument made from a hollowed-out gourd filled with seeds), and the triangle are traditional musical instruments used in Sega. These instruments work together to produce Sega music's rhythmic and hypnotic sounds.

Sega dance is distinguished by expressive movements that reflect the emotions depicted in the songs. Dancers sway their hips, move their feet to the music, and use hand gestures to convey various messages. The dance is energetic, sensual, and lively, captivating both the dancers and the audience.

Traditional Sega costumes are bright and colorful, reflecting the island's multicultural heritage. Women frequently wear long, flowing skirts with a matching top and a flower or ribbon-adorned headdress. Men typically dress in loose-fitting pants and shirts, with a straw hat or bandana on top.

Festivals and Performances: Sega dance and music are prominently featured in festivals and cultural events held in Mauritius throughout the year. The annual Festival Kreol celebrates the island's Creole culture, with Sega performances a major highlight. Sega shows are frequently featured in hotels, resorts, and beach parties, allowing visitors to experience the captivating rhythms and movements firsthand.

Cultural Importance: Sega is extremely important to the people of Mauritius. It serves as a means of preserving and celebrating the island's cultural heritage as well as a form of entertainment. The history, traditions, and stories of the Mauritian people are passed down from generation to generation through the rhythms and lyrics of Sega songs.

Experiencing Sega dance and music provides a once-in-a-lifetime opportunity to immerse oneself in Mauritius' vibrant and soulful culture. Sega offers a memorable and enriching experience that showcases the island's rich cultural tapestry, whether it's watching a live performance, joining in the dance, or simply enjoying the infectious beats.

D. Hindu Temples and Festivals

With a sizable Hindu population on the island, Hinduism plays an important role in the cultural fabric of Mauritius. As a result, Mauritius is home to numerous Hindu temples and vibrant festivals celebrating the Hindu faith. Here is a list of Hindu temples and festivals in Mauritius:

Hindu Temples:

Ganga Talao, also known as Grand Bassin, is a sacred crater lake in the Savanne district. It is the most sacred Hindu site in Mauritius and is dedicated to Lord Shiva. The lake is surrounded by several temples, including the Mahadev Temple and the Sagar Shiv Mandir, which attract both pilgrims and visitors.

Surya Deva Temple: Located in Triolet, the Surya Deva Temple is dedicated to the Sun God, Surya. It is one of the largest Hindu temples in Mauritius, with intricate architecture and stunning sculptures. The temple is a significant spiritual and cultural landmark.

The Maha Shivaratri Mandir, located in Albion, is dedicated to Lord Shiva. It is well-known for its annual Maha Shivaratri festival, during which devotees engage in night-long prayers, fasting, and spiritual rituals.

The Kali Temple, located in Port Louis, is dedicated to the Goddess Kali. It is a popular Hindu temple that draws devotees seeking the blessings and protection of the fierce deity.

Hindu Festivals:

Diwali: Diwali, also known as the Festival of Lights, is one of the most widely observed Hindu festivals in Mauritius. It represents the triumph of light over darkness and good over evil. During Diwali, homes and temples are decorated with colorful lights, and families gather to exchange gifts and share festive meals. Fireworks and the lighting of oil lamps are common traditions during this joyous occasion.

Maha Shivaratri: Maha Shivaratri is a significant festival dedicated to Lord Shiva. Devotees fast, visit temples, and participate in night-long vigils and prayers. The Maha Shivaratri celebrations at Ganga Talao attract a large number of pilgrims who embark on a sacred walk to the lake, carrying offerings and displaying their devotion.

Holi: The Hindu community in Mauritius celebrates Holi, the Festival of Colors, with enthusiasm and joy. It is a vibrant festival in which participants throw colored powders and water at each other, symbolizing the arrival of spring and the triumph of good over evil. Music, dance, and laughter fill the air.

Navaratri: Navaratri is a nine-night festival honoring the goddess Durga. It entails the worship of the divine feminine through prayer, fasting, and music. The energetic Garba and Dandiya Raas dances, in which participants form circles and dance to rhythmic beats, are the highlights of Navaratri.

These are just a few examples of Hindu temples and festivals in Mauritius. Mauritius' rich Hindu heritage and traditions allow visitors to witness and participate in colorful celebrations and spiritual practices that are deeply ingrained in the island's cultural tapestry.

E. Chinese Pagodas and Festivals

Chinese culture is prevalent in Mauritius, with a sizable Chinese community contributing to the island's multicultural tapestry. Chinese pagodas and festivals play an important role in displaying the rich traditions and customs of the Chinese community. Here's a rundown of Chinese pagodas and festivals in Mauritius:

Chinese pagodas:

Sookdeo Bissoondoyal Chinese Pagoda: Located in Port Louis, the Sookdeo Bissoondoyal Chinese Pagoda is a magnificent architectural masterpiece that features traditional Chinese design elements. It's dedicated to the Chinese deity Guan Di, also known as Kwan Tai or Guan Yu. The pagoda is a place of worship, cultural activities, and community gatherings.

China Town Pagoda: Located in Port Louis' vibrant China Town neighborhood, the China Town Pagoda is another important Chinese religious and cultural site. It is decorated with vibrant red and gold colors, intricate sculptures, and ornate decorations that reflect Chinese architectural styles. The pagoda is a prominent landmark in the bustling China Town neighborhood.

Chinese Festivals

Chinese New Year: Chinese New Year, also known as Spring Festival or Lunar New Year, is one of the most important and widely celebrated festivals among the Chinese community in Mauritius. It marks the beginning of the lunar calendar and is marked by vibrant parades, lion and dragon dances, firecrackers, and family gatherings. The streets of ChinaTown come alive with colorful decorations, traditional music, and delectable Chinese delicacies.

Lantern Festival: The Lantern Festival, held on the 15th day of the lunar calendar, marks the end of the Chinese New Year festivities. It is a joyful occasion filled with lantern displays, cultural performances, and lantern riddle-solving activities. People gather in parks and public spaces, carrying colorful lanterns and enjoying the festive atmosphere.

Moon Festival (Mid-Autumn Festival): The Chinese community celebrates the Moon Festival, also known as the Mid-Autumn Festival, in Mauritius. It's a time for family reunions and celebrating the full moon. Mooncakes, a traditional Chinese pastry filled with various sweet or savory fillings, are a popular delicacy during this festival. The evening is frequently marked by the lighting of lanterns and the exchange of mooncakes among family and friends.

Qingming Festival (Tomb-Sweeping Day): The Qingming Festival is a traditional Chinese festival that honors ancestors and pays tribute to the deceased. Families visit their ancestors' graves, clean the tombstones, and make offerings of food, flowers, and incense. It is a time for reflection, remembrance, and honoring family heritage.

These are some of the Chinese pagodas and festivals celebrated in Mauritius. The vibrant cultural heritage of the Chinese community adds to the island's multicultural fabric, providing visitors with the opportunity to witness and participate in the colorful traditions and festivities that are an integral part of Chinese culture in Mauritius.

F. Muslim Mosques and Festivals

Mauritius has a sizable Muslim minority, and Islamic culture plays an important role in the island's cultural variety. Mosques and Islamic holidays are very important to the Muslim community. Here is a list of Muslim mosques and festivals in Mauritius:

Muslim Mosques:

Jummah Masjid: Located in the capital city of Port Louis, the Jummah Masjid is one of Mauritius' most important and historic mosques. It is a focal point for the Muslim community and serves as a place of worship and community meeting. The mosque has amazing architecture and exquisite embellishments.

Jummah Mosque: Located in the village of Curepipe, the Jummah Mosque is another important Islamic religious landmark in Mauritius. It is well-known for its huge prayer hall and minaret, and it serves as a center for Friday prayers and Islamic lectures.

Noor-e-Islam Mosque: The Noor-e-Islam Mosque, located in the village of Saint-Pierre, is a lovely mosque with stunning architecture. It draws both believers and visitors, offering a tranquil setting for meditation and reflection.

Muslim Festivals:

Eid al-Fitr: Eid al-Fitr, also known as the Festival of Breaking the Fast, marks the end of Ramadan, the Islamic holy month of fasting. Muslims mark the occasion with special prayers, family gatherings, and feasts. It is a cheerful celebration, with people exchanging gifts and donating to charity. The environment is one of community, forgiveness, and thanks.

Eid al-Adha: Eid al-Adha, also known as the Festival of Sacrifice, honors Ibrahim's (Abraham's) willingness to sacrifice his son as an act of obedience to God. Muslims congregate for prayers, sermons, and animal sacrifice, with the meat handed to the poor. It is a time for introspection, gratitude, and charity.

Mawlid al-Nabi: Mawlid al-Nabi commemorates the birth of the Islamic prophet Muhammad. Muslims commemorate this day with prayers, Quran recitation, and gatherings where stories about the Prophet's life and teachings are recounted. It is a moment of recollection and devotion.

Laylat al-Qadr, also known as the Night of Power, is regarded as one of the holiest evenings in the Islamic calendar. It commemorates the night when the first words of the Quran were revealed to the Prophet Muhammad. Muslims pray fervently, seeking spiritual benefits and forgiveness. It is a night of serious meditation, dedication, and petition.

These are some of the mosques and festivals celebrated by the Muslim community in Mauritius. Islamic customs and cultural practices enrich the island's diverse multicultural landscape, allowing tourists to experience and appreciate the island's rich Islamic legacy.

G. Diwali Festival of Lights

Diwali, also known as the Festival of Lights, is one of Mauritius' most important and widely celebrated festivals. It is extremely culturally and religiously significant for the Hindu community, as well as other communities that participate in the festivities. Here's a rundown of Diwali in Mauritius:

Diwali Celebrations:

Diya lighting: Diwali is marked by the lighting of diyas (oil lamps) in homes, temples, and public places. The soft glow of the diyas creates a spellbinding atmosphere, symbolizing the triumph of light over darkness and good over evil.

Decorations: Rangoli patterns made of colored powders or flowers adorn homes and businesses. To welcome prosperity and good fortune, intricate designs and patterns are created.

Fireworks are an essential part of Diwali celebrations. Fireworks spectacularly light up the sky, adding excitement and joy to the festive atmosphere. People of all ages gather to witness and enjoy the hypnotic spectacle.

Family Get-Togethers: Diwali is a time for families to gather and celebrate. Friends and relatives pay each other visits, exchange gifts, and share special meals. It is a time of joy, love, and community.

Delicious Sweets: Diwali isn't complete unless you indulge in a variety of delectable sweets and snacks. Traditional desserts such as gulab jamun, barfi, ladoos, and jalebis are made and shared with family and friends.

Religious significance:

Diwali is associated with several religious legends. One of the most well-known stories is Lord Rama's return to his kingdom of Ayodhya after 14 years in exile, accompanied by his wife Sita and brother Lakshmana. To commemorate their return, people lit up the entire city with earthen lamps, establishing the origins of Diwali.

During Diwali, Hindus pray to Goddess Lakshmi, the goddess of wealth and prosperity, for a prosperous year ahead. At home and in temples, prayers and offerings are made.

Diwali is also associated with the celebration of Lord Krishna's victory over the demon Narakasura, which symbolizes the triumph of good over evil.

Diwali is a time of joy, unity, and spiritual reflection in Mauritius. It exemplifies the island's diversity and multiculturalism as people from various communities come together to celebrate this auspicious occasion. The Festival of Lights energizes the island and serves as a reminder of the triumph of light and goodness in our lives.

Chapter 6: Adventure and Outdoor Activities

A. Hiking and Trekking

For outdoor enthusiasts, Mauritius has some excellent hiking and trekking opportunities. The island's varied landscapes, which include mountains, forests, and coastal areas, offer a variety of options for hikers of varying levels of experience. Here are some of the most popular hiking and trekking spots in Mauritius:

Le Morne Brabant is a UNESCO World Heritage Site and a popular hiking destination. This iconic mountain is located on the island's southwestern tip and provides breathtaking panoramic views of the surrounding ocean. The ascent is difficult but rewarding, with breathtaking views and a glimpse into Mauritius' history.

Black River Gorges National Park: The Black River Gorges National Park is a hiker's paradise and one of Mauritius' most significant natural areas. Numerous trails in the park lead through lush forests, cascading waterfalls, and scenic overlooks. Hikers looking for adventure and beautiful vistas should consider the Macchabee Trail and the Black River Peak Trail.

Tamarin Falls: Tamarin Falls is a picturesque waterfall surrounded by verdant forests near the village of Tamarin. Hiking to Tamarin Falls allows visitors to appreciate nature's beauty, discover hidden pools, and cool off in the crystal-clear waters.

The Seven Cascades (Tamarind Falls): The Seven Cascades, also known as Tamarind Falls, are a series of waterfalls located in Mauritius's heart. This area has thrilling hiking trails through rugged terrain, lush vegetation, and breathtaking scenery. The hike includes river crossings, rock climbing, and breathtaking views of the cascades.

Lion Mountain (Montagne du Lion) is a popular hiking destination in the southern part of Mauritius. The summit trail provides panoramic views of the coastline and surrounding countryside. The hike can be difficult, but it is well worth it for the breathtaking views.

Bras d'Eau National Park: Located on Mauritius' northeastern coast, Bras d'Eau National Park offers scenic trails through mangrove forests, coastal dunes, and wetlands. The park is a paradise for birdwatchers and nature lovers, with opportunities to see endemic bird species and other wildlife.

Domaine de Chazal: Domaine de Chazal is a private nature reserve in Mauritius' south. Hiking trails in the reserve include a panoramic ridge hike and a trek to a hidden waterfall. Hikers can use the trails to explore the area's unique flora and fauna.

These hiking and trekking destinations in Mauritius allow outdoor enthusiasts to discover hidden gems and experience the tranquillity of nature while exploring the island's natural wonders. Whether you're a novice or a seasoned hiker, there are options for all levels of fitness and adventure.

B. Quad Biking and Off-Roading

Quad biking and off-roading in Mauritius provide thrilling and adventurous experiences for those looking to explore the island's rugged terrain and natural landscapes. Whether you're a beginner or an experienced rider, this adrenaline-pumping activity is an exciting way to discover hidden gems. Here's what you can expect from quad biking and off-roading in Mauritius.

For starters, quad biking and off-roading provide an adrenaline rush as you navigate through difficult terrain, maneuvering your quad bike over bumps, hills, and uneven surfaces. Quad biking is an unforgettable experience due to the thrill of speed and the thrill of overcoming obstacles.

Second, Mauritius has stunning natural beauty, and quad biking allows you to explore picturesque landscapes. Ride through sugar cane fields, dense forests, and off-the-beaten-path trails, immersing yourself in a variety of environments. As you travel into less-explored areas, you will be treated to breathtaking views of mountains, valleys, rivers, and coastlines.

Finally, quad biking and off-roading cater to riders of various skill levels. Whether you're a novice or a seasoned rider, there are options to suit your skill level. Guided tours with trained instructors ensure your safety while guiding you through the best routes and pointing out interesting sights along the way.

Furthermore, quad biking is frequently enjoyed in groups, making it a social and entertaining activity. Gather your friends or join a group tour to share the excitement and make lasting memories. Experience camaraderie as you ride together, exchanging laughs and thrills while exploring the island's landscapes.

Furthermore, quad biking in Mauritius provides a unique opportunity to immerse yourself in the local culture and way of life. Pass through villages, interact with locals, and observe their daily activities. This cultural immersion enriches your quad-biking adventure.

Furthermore, quad biking is an excellent activity for families with older children or teenagers. It allows you to bond as a family while taking an exhilarating journey through nature. Many operators provide family-friendly quad biking tours with appropriate routes and safety precautions.

Finally, off-roading takes you away from the traditional roads and into the heart of Mauritius' untamed landscapes. Traverse muddy paths, rocky terrain, and difficult obstacles to put your driving skills to the test. It's an off-road adventure that promises excitement and a sense of accomplishment.

Finally, quad biking and off-roading in Mauritius combine adventure, exploration, and natural beauty. With diverse landscapes and knowledgeable guides, you can embark on an unforgettable journey that combines adrenaline, breathtaking scenery, and cultural encounters. So suit up, hop on a quad bike, and prepare for an off-road adventure unlike any other.

C. Ziplining and Canyoning

In Mauritius, ziplining and canyoning provide thrilling and adventurous experiences that allow you to explore the island's natural wonders in novel ways.

Ziplining allows you to soar through the air and see Mauritius' breathtaking landscapes from a whole new perspective. Strapped into a harness, you'll float along steel cables suspended between platforms, taking in the island's lush forests, dramatic gorges, and sparkling coastlines. Ziplining is an unforgettable adventure because of the adrenaline rush of zipping through the air at high speeds and the unique perspectives it provides.

Canyoning, on the other hand, takes you on an exciting journey through the canyons of the island, where you'll navigate waterfalls, rock formations, and natural pools. Descending through cascading waterfalls, abseiling down cliffs, jumping into clear pools, and sliding down natural water slides, you'll feel the rush of adventure while immersed in the natural beauty of Mauritius. Canyoning allows you to explore hidden gorges, swim in crystal-clear pools, and get up close and personal with the surrounding flora and fauna.

Both ziplining and canyoning offer a rush of adrenaline, breathtaking scenery, and intimate encounters with nature. Whether you choose to fly through the air or descend through canyons, these activities provide unique perspectives, thrilling experiences, and unforgettable memories on Mauritius' beautiful island.

D. Golfing in Mauritius

Golf in Mauritius is a delightful experience for those who enjoy this elegant sport. Mauritius has become a popular golf destination due to its breathtaking landscapes, world-class golf courses, and tropical climate. Here's what to expect if you go golfing in Mauritius.

To begin with, Mauritius has an impressive collection of golf courses designed by well-known architects. These courses make the most of the island's natural beauty, with lush green fairways, palm-fringed lakes, and breathtaking coastal views. Each course has its own distinct personality, offering a challenging yet enjoyable golfing experience.

Second, Mauritius' tropical climate allows for year-round golfing opportunities. The mild temperatures, gentle sea breeze, and abundant sunshine make for ideal golf conditions. You can expect pleasant weather whether you visit in the summer or winter, which will enhance your golfing experience.

Third, Mauritius' golf courses cater to golfers of all skill levels, from beginners to professionals. Whether you're a seasoned player looking to put your skills to the test or a beginner looking to improve, you'll find courses to suit your needs. Many courses provide professional instruction and practice areas, allowing you to fine-tune your swing and technique.

Furthermore, golfing in Mauritius allows you to immerse yourself in breathtaking scenery. You'll be treated to panoramic views of the Indian Ocean, rolling hills, and tropical vegetation as you navigate the fairways. The beauty of the courses adds to the overall golf experience and creates a relaxing atmosphere.

Furthermore, many Mauritius golf resorts provide world-class amenities and services. Everything you need for a comfortable and enjoyable golfing experience is available, from luxurious clubhouses to well-equipped pro shops. After your game, relax and rejuvenate at the resort's restaurants and bars, or indulge in spa treatments.

Furthermore, golf can be combined with other activities in Mauritius to create a well-rounded vacation. Explore the island's natural wonders, participate in water sports, or simply relax on pristine beaches. There is something for everyone, whether they are golfers or accompanying family members, thanks to the diverse range of leisure options.

Finally, golfing in Mauritius combines beautiful landscapes, well-designed courses, and a pleasant climate to create a memorable experience for golf enthusiasts. The island's golf courses cater to all skill levels, whether you're a beginner or an experienced player. Mauritius is a golfer's paradise waiting to be discovered, with its tropical beauty, luxurious amenities, and opportunities for relaxation and adventure.

E. Kiteboarding and Windsurfing

Mauritius' kiteboarding and windsurfing provide thrilling water sports experiences for adventure seekers. Mauritius has become a popular destination for these thrilling activities due to its favorable wind conditions, warm waters, and beautiful coastlines. Here's what to expect if you go kiteboarding or windsurfing in Mauritius.

For starters, Mauritius has ideal wind conditions for kiteboarding and windsurfing all year. The consistent trade winds, especially from May to October, provide a steady breeze that allows for exciting rides and excellent control over the equipment. The geographic features of the island, such as its lagoons and offshore reefs, create favorable wind patterns, making it a haven for wind-driven water sports.

Second, the warm and clear waters of Mauritius are ideal for kiteboarding and windsurfing. The turquoise lagoons provide spacious riding areas with shallow depths and sandy bottoms, ensuring a safe and enjoyable ride. The tropical climate of Mauritius adds to the allure, allowing you to participate in these activities all year.

Third, Mauritius has become a kiteboarding and windsurfing mecca, attracting enthusiasts from all over the world. Numerous kiteboarding and windsurfing centers on the island offer equipment rental, lessons, and expert guidance to both beginners and advanced riders. Whether you're a beginner looking to learn or an experienced rider looking for new challenges, professional instructors and well-equipped facilities will meet your needs.

Furthermore, Mauritius' coastlines provide a variety of kiteboarding and windsurfing spots, each with its own distinct characteristics. There's something for everyone, from the flat-water lagoons of Le Morne and Anse La Raie to the more challenging wave spots of One Eye and Tamarin Bay. These diverse locations allow you to hone your skills, try new techniques, and experience a variety of riding conditions.

Furthermore, kiteboarding and windsurfing in Mauritius provides a unique perspective on the island's natural beauty. Glide over the crystal-clear waters, experience an adrenaline rush as you catch the wind, and take in panoramic views of the coastline, coral reefs, and surrounding landscapes. It's an exhilarating way to connect with nature and discover Mauritius' natural beauty.

In addition, the kiteboarding and windsurfing communities in Mauritius are active and welcoming. Whether you're riding alone or with friends, you'll find a welcoming and supportive environment among fellow enthusiasts. As you immerse yourself in Mauritius' dynamic water sports scene, share your experiences, exchange tips, and make new connections.

Finally, kiteboarding and windsurfing in Mauritius provide exciting water sports experiences in a beautiful tropical setting. The island is an ideal playground for kiteboarders and windsurfers, with favorable wind conditions, warm waters, and a variety of spots catering to different skill levels. Mauritius invites you to harness the wind, ride the waves, and create unforgettable memories in its beautiful waters, whether you're a beginner or an expert.

F. Deep-Sea Fishing

Deep-sea fishing in Mauritius is an exciting and rewarding experience for anglers. Mauritius has earned a reputation as a top destination for deep-sea fishing due to its rich marine biodiversity, abundant fishing grounds, and favorable oceanic conditions. Here's what to expect if you decide to go deep-sea fishing in Mauritius:

For starters, Mauritius has a diverse range of fish species that live in its deep waters. The island's fishing grounds are teeming with opportunities to land impressive catches, including prized big game fish like marlin, sailfish, and tuna, as well as other popular catches like Dorado, wahoo, and Barracuda. Deep-sea fishing in Mauritius is a truly unforgettable experience because of the challenge and excitement of reeling in these powerful fish.

Second, Mauritius benefits from its strategic location in the Indian Ocean, where oceanic conditions are favorable for deep-sea fishing. Warm currents, underwater canyons, and offshore reefs all contribute to the thriving marine ecosystem, attracting a diverse range of fish species. The oceanic drop-offs near the coast are ideal for fishing because they provide a transition zone where large predatory fish congregate.

Third, experienced fishing charters and guides can enhance your deep-sea fishing experience in Mauritius. These experts are well-versed in the local fishing grounds, techniques, and best practices. They can advise you on baiting, trolling, and locating hotspots for various fish species, increasing your chances of having a successful fishing trip.

Deep-sea fishing charters in Mauritius are also outfitted with well-maintained boats, high-quality fishing gear, and the necessary safety equipment. They cater to both novice and seasoned anglers, ensuring a relaxing and enjoyable fishing experience. You can tailor your fishing adventure to your preferences, whether you prefer a full-day excursion or a half-day trip.

Furthermore, deep-sea fishing in Mauritius provides not only the thrill of the catch but also the opportunity to take in the island's breathtaking coastal scenery. As you dive into the deep waters, you'll be surrounded by panoramic views of the Indian Ocean and the stunning coastline. The tranquil setting and sense of being one with nature enhance the overall experience.

Mauritius also hosts several fishing tournaments and events throughout the year, attracting anglers from all over the world. These competitions highlight the island's vibrant fishing culture while also providing opportunities to compete and connect with other fishermen. Participating in a fishing tournament in Mauritius can add excitement to your deep-sea fishing trip.

Finally, deep-sea fishing in Mauritius is an exhilarating and rewarding adventure for anglers. Mauritius provides the ideal setting for an unforgettable fishing experience, with its diverse fish species, favorable oceanic conditions, experienced fishing charters, and breathtaking coastal scenery. Whether you're a seasoned angler looking for big game fish or a novice looking to try your hand at deep-sea fishing, Mauritius invites you to cast your line, feel the thrill of the catch, and create lasting memories on the Indian Ocean's open waters.

Chapter 7: Shopping and Souvenirs

A. Local Handicrafts and Artwork

Mauritius is well-known for its handicrafts and artwork, which provide a unique insight into the island's culture, creativity, and craftsmanship. Here's what to expect when exploring local handicrafts and artwork in Mauritius, from traditional crafts passed down through generations to contemporary artwork inspired by the island's beauty.

To begin, textiles play an important role in Mauritian craftsmanship. The island is famous for its colorful and intricately designed textiles, such as the well-known "batik" and "madras" fabrics. Batik is a dyeing technique that uses wax to create beautiful patterns and designs on fabric. With its vibrant plaid patterns, Madras fabric is frequently used in traditional clothing and accessories. Textiles ranging from sarongs and dresses to bags and home decor items are available, showcasing the artistic expertise of local artisans.

Second, woodcarving is a popular craft in Mauritius. Local woods are transformed into intricate sculptures, decorative objects, and furniture by skilled artisans. Wooden artworks reflect the island's natural beauty and rich heritage, ranging from delicate figurines to larger sculptures depicting local wildlife and cultural symbols. These handcrafted wooden pieces make for one-of-a-kind and meaningful keepsakes.

Third, basketry is a centuries-old traditional craft practiced in Mauritius. Local artisans weave baskets, mats, and decorative items from various materials such as straw, cane, and palm leaves. These woven products showcase the artisans' craftsmanship and creativity while also serving practical purposes. Basketry items that add a touch of Mauritian charm to your home or serve as memorable gifts are available.

Furthermore, Mauritian art spans a wide range of styles and mediums. Many artists are inspired by the natural beauty of the island, incorporating vibrant colors and intricate details into their paintings, sculptures, and mixed-media works. The artwork frequently reflects Mauritius' multicultural heritage, depicting scenes of local life, landscapes, and cultural traditions. Art galleries and studios offer the opportunity to discover and purchase original works by talented Mauritius artists.

Ceramics and pottery are also highly valued forms of artistic expression in Mauritius. Ceramic pieces made by skilled potters range from decorative vases and bowls to functional tableware. The ceramics frequently feature intricate designs, hand-painted motifs, and vibrant glazes, showcasing the artists' craftsmanship and creativity. These ceramics make unique and eye-catching additions to your home or thoughtful gifts for loved ones.

Furthermore, Mauritian artisans' jewelry is highly regarded for its unique designs and use of local materials. From colorful beaded necklaces and bracelets to silver or gold pieces with gemstones, the jewelry reflects the island's cultural diversity and natural resources. Local markets, craft shops, and jewelry boutiques sell a wide variety of handcrafted jewelry, allowing you to take a piece of Mauritius with you wherever you go.

Finally, Mauritius has a rich tradition of local handicrafts and artwork that captures the island's culture, heritage, and natural surroundings. There are numerous opportunities to explore and acquire unique pieces crafted by talented Mauritian artisans, ranging from textiles and woodcarving to basketry, ceramics, and jewelry. These handicrafts and artworks serve as souvenirs as well as a meaningful connection to the island's creativity, craftsmanship, and vibrant cultural identity.

B. Clothing and Accessories

Mauritius has a wide range of clothing and accessories that reflect the island's style, culture, and climate. Here's what you can find in Mauritius if you're looking for beachwear, resort wear, or unique accessories.

To begin, beachwear is a popular choice in Mauritius due to its beautiful coastlines and year-round warm weather. Local shops and beachside stalls sell a variety of swimsuits, bikinis, board shorts, and cover-ups. Beachwear options range from vibrant prints and tropical motifs to stylish designs to suit a variety of tastes and preferences.

Second, resort wear is a Mauritius staple, catering to the island's tourism industry. Flowy dresses, lightweight tops, linen pants, and elegant kaftans are among the stylish clothing options suitable for luxury resorts. These pieces frequently feature relaxed silhouettes, breathable fabrics, and tropical-inspired designs.

Third, traditional Mauritian clothing is worth investigating if you want to learn about the island's cultural heritage. The "sagas" dress, a traditional Creole outfit, is colorful and vibrant attire that is frequently worn at festivals and cultural events. It usually consists of a long, flowing dress with ruffled sleeves and a floral-patterned headscarf. Shell necklaces and beaded bracelets are traditional accessories that go well with the outfit.

Mauritius is also known for its textile industry, which produces high-quality fabrics with distinctive designs. Textiles from the island, including batik and madras fabrics, are used in a variety of clothing items, including shirts, skirts, and scarves. These fabrics are distinctive and representative of Mauritian craftsmanship because they frequently feature bright colors, intricate patterns, and cultural motifs.

Furthermore, accessories are important in completing a stylish look, and Mauritius has a variety of options. Handmade jewelry made from local materials such as shells, beads, and semi-precious stones reflects the natural beauty of the island. Necklaces, bracelets, earrings, and rings are available that showcase the creativity and talent of Mauritian artisans.

Straw hats, woven bags, and beach towels are also practical and fashionable beach accessories for a Mauritius beach vacation. These items are frequently handcrafted from natural materials such as straw, sisal, or raffia, and will add a touch of island style to your ensemble. They can be found at local markets and beachside stalls.

Finally, Mauritius has a wide variety of clothing and accessories to suit various styles, occasions, and preferences. Whether you're looking for beachwear, resort wear, traditional clothing, or one-of-a-kind accessories, the island has plenty to offer. Discover clothing and accessories that reflect the island's vibrant culture, natural beauty, and relaxed lifestyle by exploring local shops, markets, and boutique stores.

C. Local Rum and Tea

Mauritius is well-known for its rum and tea production, both of which showcase the island's rich agricultural heritage and craftsmanship. Here's everything you need to know about Mauritius' rum and tea.

To begin, local rum has a special place in the culture and history of Mauritius. The island has a long history of rum production dating back to the days of sugarcane plantations. Today, visitors to the island can visit various rum distilleries to learn about the rum-making process and sample a variety of flavors and blends.

Mauritian rum is known for its distinct flavor, which is often influenced by the tropical climate and terroir of the island. The rum is made from sugarcane grown locally, which is harvested, crushed, and fermented to produce a molasses-based distillate. It is then aged in oak barrels for several years, allowing the flavors to develop and mature.

There are numerous Mauritian rums available, ranging from white or light rums to dark and aged rums. Each category has its own distinct personality and can be consumed neat, on the rocks, or in tropical cocktails. Rhum de Chamarel, Penny Blue, and New Grove are some of the most popular rum brands in Mauritius.

Mauritius is also well-known for its tea production, which thrives on the island's fertile volcanic soil and mild climate. Tea plantations can be found in Mauritius' central and southern regions, allowing visitors to explore the estates and learn about the tea-making process.

Mauritian tea is well-known for its high quality and diverse flavor profiles. To preserve the aroma and flavor of the tea leaves, they are hand-picked and processed. There are numerous tea varieties available, including black tea, green tea, and herbal infusions. Bois Chéri and Domaine des Aubineaux are two popular Mauritian tea brands.

Visiting a tea plantation or tea factory allows you to see how tea leaves are harvested, processed, and packaged firsthand. You can also attend tea tastings to sample different teas and discover your favorite flavors.

Local rum and tea are both excellent souvenirs or gifts to bring back from Mauritius. Many distilleries and tea estates have onsite shops where you can buy rum bottles, tea bags, loose-leaf tea, and other related products. These local beverages allow you to savor Mauritius' flavors long after your visit.

Finally, Mauritius' rum and tea are highly valued for their exceptional quality and reflect the island's agricultural heritage. Exploring the world of Mauritian rum and tea is a delightful experience, whether you are a rum enthusiast or a tea lover. You can enjoy the flavors and aromas of Mauritius wherever you are by sampling different rums and teas, visiting distilleries and tea estates, and purchasing bottles or packs to bring back home.

D. Shopping Malls and Boutiques

Mauritius has a thriving shopping scene, complete with shopping malls and boutiques where you can indulge in retail therapy. Whether you're looking for international brands, local designs, or one-of-a-kind handicrafts, here's what to expect when visiting Mauritius' shopping malls and boutiques.

Shopping Malls: Mauritius has several modern shopping malls that cater to a wide range of shopping preferences. These malls offer a convenient and comfortable shopping experience, often with a diverse selection of international and local brands, dining options, entertainment facilities, and other amenities. Bagatelle Mall of Mauritius, Phoenix Mall, Trianon Shopping Park, and Cascavelle Shopping Village are some of the most popular shopping malls in Mauritius. These shopping centers house a wide range of stores, including fashion boutiques, electronics stores, beauty outlets, and specialty stores, allowing you to find everything from clothing and accessories to home decor and electronics.

Boutiques: Exploring boutiques is a must for a more unique and curated shopping experience. Mauritius is home to several boutique shops that feature local designs, craftsmanship, and emerging fashion trends. These shops frequently sell locally made clothing, accessories, and home decor items that showcase the island's creativity and style. Boutiques offer a chance to discover one-of-a-kind pieces that reflect Mauritius' cultural heritage and contemporary aesthetics, ranging from handmade garments and jewelry to artisanal crafts and artworks. The waterfront promenades in Port Louis and Grand Baie, as well as the trendy streets of Flic en Flac and Tamarin, are all popular boutique areas.

Local Markets: Exploring local markets, in addition to malls and boutiques, is an important part of the shopping experience in Mauritius. Markets with a vibrant atmosphere, such as the Central Market in Port Louis and the Flacq Market, offer a diverse range of products. Fresh produce, spices, souvenirs, clothing, accessories, and handicrafts can all be found here. Negotiating prices is common in these markets, so be prepared to do so for a more authentic shopping experience. Local markets also allow you to interact with friendly vendors while immersing yourself in the island's vibrant culture.

Mauritius is well-known for its artisanal villages, which are dedicated to showcasing traditional craftsmanship and local products. These villages, such as Curepipe's Craft Market and Le Caudan Waterfront Craft Market, offer a treasure trove of handcrafted items such as woven baskets, wooden sculptures, pottery, textiles, and more. Exploring these artisanal villages allows you to directly support local artisans, learn about their techniques, and bring home one-of-a-kind and authentic souvenirs representing Mauritius' cultural heritage.

Finally, with a variety of shopping malls, boutiques, local markets, and artisanal villages, Mauritius provides a diverse shopping experience. Whether you're looking for international brands, local designs, or one-of-a-kind handicrafts, you'll find plenty of options. Exploring the shopping scene in Mauritius allows you to discover hidden gems, indulge in retail therapy, and bring home memorable souvenirs that capture the essence of the island, from upscale malls and trendy boutiques to bustling markets and artisanal villages.

E. Duty-Free Shopping

Mauritius has a thriving duty-free shopping experience, allowing visitors to take advantage of tax-free prices on a wide range of products. Duty-free shopping in Mauritius allows you to indulge in retail therapy at a lower cost, whether you're looking for luxury items, electronics, cosmetics, or souvenirs. Here's everything you need to know about shopping duty-free in Mauritius.

Duty-Free Shops: Duty-free shops are located at Mauritius' main international airports, including Sir Seewoosagur Ramgoolam International Airport in Plaine Magnien. These shops are conveniently located within airport terminals and offer a wide range of duty-free items. Fashion, accessories, watches, jewelry, and fragrances are among the luxury brands available. Electronics such as cameras, smartphones, and tablets are also available duty-free. Duty-free shops also sell cosmetics, skincare products, spirits, wines, and tobacco products.

Tax-Free Allowances: It is critical to understand the tax-free allowances and regulations when shopping duty-free in Mauritius. The duty-free allowance for Mauritius, as of September 2021, is 250 grams of tobacco or 200 cigarettes, 1 liter of spirits, 2 liters of wine, and up to 2 liters of beer per person. These allowances are subject to change, so check the most recent regulations before traveling to ensure compliance.

Souvenirs and Local Products: In addition to luxury items and electronics, Mauritius duty-free shops sell a variety of local products and souvenirs. Traditional handicrafts, textiles, artwork, and local food products make excellent souvenirs or gifts. These items allow you to bring a piece of Mauritius' cultural heritage home while benefiting from duty-free prices.

VAT Refunds: If you make purchases outside of duty-free stores, you may be eligible for VAT refunds. Some Mauritius stores participate in the VAT refund scheme, allowing tourists to claim a refund on eligible purchases. To be eligible for a VAT refund, you must follow the necessary procedures and meet the criteria established by the Mauritian authorities. Keep in mind that each store may have different requirements for VAT refunds, so it's best to check with the retailer directly at the time of purchase.

Finally, duty-free shopping in Mauritius provides an exciting opportunity to purchase luxury items, electronics, cosmetics, and souvenirs at tax-free prices. Duty-free shops at international airports offer travelers a convenient shopping experience. Remember to familiarize yourself with the tax-free allowances and regulations, as well as any applicable VAT refund schemes. Duty-free shopping in Mauritius allows you to enjoy the pleasure of shopping while potentially saving on taxes, whether you're looking for high-end brands, local products, or unique souvenirs.

Chapter 8: Practical Information for Mauritius visitors

A. Health and Safety Tips

It is critical to take the necessary health and safety precautions when planning a trip to Mauritius. Here are some important rules to remember:

Medical Preparations: Make your health a priority by meeting with a healthcare professional or a travel clinic before your trip to discuss necessary vaccinations and medications.

Purchase comprehensive travel insurance that includes coverage for medical expenses, emergency medical evacuation, and trip cancellation/interruption.

Sun Protection: Wear sunscreen with a high SPF, a wide-brimmed hat, and sunglasses to protect yourself from the tropical sun. During the hottest hours of the day, seek shade.

Water and Food Safety: To avoid drinking tap water, drink bottled water or use a water purifier. Consume food with caution and only from reputable establishments.

Mosquito-Borne Diseases: Avoid mosquito bites by using repellents, wearing long-sleeved clothing, and staying in accommodations that have been properly screened.

Beach and Water Safety: When swimming, follow safety guidelines and pay attention to beach warning signs. Swim in designated areas where lifeguards are on duty.

Personal Safety: Be cautious and aware of your surroundings. Keep an eye on your belongings and stay away from poorly lit or isolated areas, particularly at night.

COVID-19 Precautions: Keep up-to-date on the most recent COVID-19 travel restrictions, entry requirements, and health protocols. Follow local guidelines, wear masks, maintain proper hand hygiene, and practice social distancing.
Keep up to date:

Keep up-to-date on travel advisories or warnings issued by the government of your home country or international organizations.
You can ensure a safe and enjoyable visit to Mauritius by following these health and safety guidelines.

B. Local Customs and Etiquette

When visiting Mauritius, it is important to be aware of the local customs and etiquette to respect the country's culture and traditions. Here are some key points to remember:

Handshakes are appropriate when meeting someone for the first time. Friends and family may greet each other with a kiss on the cheek in more casual settings.
When addressing people, use respectful titles such as "Mr." or "Mrs." until they are invited to use their first names.

Clothing: Although the dress code in Mauritius is relatively relaxed, it is recommended that visitors dress modestly, especially when visiting religious sites or rural areas.
Remove your shoes and dress modestly when visiting temples, mosques, or other places of worship, covering your shoulders and knees.

Politeness: In Mauritian culture, politeness is highly valued. Say "hello" and "goodbye" as you enter and exit stores, restaurants, and other establishments.

Respect elders and authority figures, and use "please" and "thank you" when communicating with locals.

Mauritius is well-known for its diverse culinary traditions. It is customary to bring a small gift or dessert as a token of appreciation when invited to someone's home for a meal.

Try to sample local dishes while remaining mindful of others' dietary restrictions or preferences.

Languages: English, French, and Mauritian Creole are the official languages of Mauritius. Although English is widely spoken, learning a few basic Creole or French phrases will be appreciated by locals.

Mauritius is a multi-religious country that practices Hinduism, Christianity, Islam, and Buddhism.

Respect religious sites and customs, and obtain permission before photographing them.

Tipping: Tipping is not required in Mauritius, but it is customary to leave a small tip for excellent service at restaurants, hotels, or other establishments.

While Mauritian society is generally tolerant, it is best to be discreet with public displays of affection, as overly affectionate behavior may be perceived as inappropriate in some contexts.

Environmental Concerns: Mauritius is very proud of its natural beauty. Respect the environment by not littering and keeping conservation efforts in mind.

You can have a more culturally sensitive and enjoyable experience in Mauritius if you are aware of these customs and etiquette.

C. Useful Phrases in Mauritian Creole

Here are some useful Mauritian Creole phrases to help you communicate with locals and have a better experience in Mauritius:

Bonzour (Bohn-zoor) - Good day / Good morning
Bonswar (Bohn-swahr) - Evening / Night
Merci (Mehr-see) - Thank you very much.
If or plé (As seen in oo play) - Could you please call
Koman? (Koh-mahn oo ah-pell) - Can you tell me your name?

Mo appel... (Moo ah-pell) - I'm Ki manier. (Kee mahn-yay) - How are things going for you?
Très bien, meri (Moo byen, mehr-see) - No problem, Kuma sa pé dir? What does that mean (Koo-mah sah pay deer)?
Konpran (Kohn-prahn): I get it.

I don't understand "Moo pa konpran (Moo pah kohn-prahn).

Kitsozé (Keet-soh-zay) - Please excuse my French.

Yes Bwi (Bwee) Non (Nohn) No Kouma (Koo-mah) - How are you, Kifer? (Kee-fair) - What's the deal?

What Kote is Ki (Kee)? (Koh-tay) - Where are you?

Kisanla? (Kee-san-lah) - How much does it cost?

Good appetite (Bohn ah-peh-tee) - Good appetite

Always remember to greet locals with a smile and a friendly attitude. Even if you only know a few basic phrases, attempting to speak Mauritian Creole will be appreciated by the locals and can help make your visit to Mauritius more enjoyable and immersive.

D. Emergency Contacts

It is critical to be prepared for emergencies in Mauritius by knowing the relevant contact numbers. Dial 999 for immediate assistance in the event of a police emergency. Call 114 if you have a medical emergency or need an ambulance. In the event of a fire or if you require rescue assistance, dial

995. If you are a tourist looking for information or assistance, call the Tourism Information Hotline at 152. It is also advisable to have the contact information for your country's consulate or embassy on hand in case you require their assistance. Remember to keep these emergency numbers handy and to be aware of your surroundings to ensure your safety during your stay in Mauritius.

E. Internet and Connectivity

Here is some important information to know about the internet and connectivity in Mauritius:

Mobile Network Coverage: Mauritius has a well-developed mobile network infrastructure that provides island-wide coverage. Mauritius' major mobile network operators are Orange, Emtel, and MTML (Chili). These providers sell local SIM cards that can be used to access mobile data and make local calls.

Wi-Fi Availability: Many Mauritius hotels, resorts, restaurants, cafes, and public spaces provide free Wi-Fi to their customers. Wi-Fi is widely available in tourist areas, shopping malls, and airports. However, the Wi-Fi connection's quality and speed may vary.

Internet Cafes: Internet cafes can be found in urban areas as well as popular tourist destinations. These businesses charge a fee for computer and internet access. They can be useful if you don't have a mobile device or require a consistent internet connection.

Roaming and International Plans: Before traveling to Mauritius, check with your mobile service provider about international roaming options and data plans. This allows you to stay connected while avoiding high roaming fees. Some service providers sell international data packages that you can buy for the duration of your trip.

Public Wi-Fi Security: Use caution when connecting to public Wi-Fi networks and avoid accessing sensitive information or conducting financial transactions. For added security, consider using a virtual private network (VPN).

Internet Access: Internet access in Mauritius is generally reliable, particularly in urban areas. It is important to note, however, that the speed will vary depending on your location and the service provider.

Online Services and Apps: Mauritius has many popular online services and apps, such as ride-hailing platforms, food delivery apps, and travel booking platforms. Before your trip, make sure to download the necessary apps and check their availability.

You can access information, stay in touch with loved ones, and make the most of your travel experience by staying connected to the internet in Mauritius.

Chapter 9: Emergency Contacts and Useful Resources

A. Embassies and Consulates

Here are some Mauritius embassies and consulates:

United States of America Embassy

Rogers House is located on John Kennedy Street in Port Louis.
+230 202 4400; email: ptlconsular@state.gov
URL: mu.usembassy.gov

India's High Commission

Contact: +230 208 3775 / 208 3776 Email: hoc.portlouis@mea.gov.in Website: www.hcimauritius.gov.in Address: 6th Floor, Life Insurance Corporation of India (LIC) Building, President John Kennedy Street, Port Louis Address:

6th Floor, Life Insurance Corporation of India (LIC) Building, President John Kennedy Street, Port Louis

United Kingdom High Commission

Rogers House, 2nd Floor, John Kennedy Street, Port Louis
Phone: +230 202 9400
Contact us at ukinmauritius@fco.gov.uk.
Website:
https://www.gov.uk/government/world/organizations/british-high-commission-port-louis

Australia High Commission

Rogers House, 2nd Floor, John Kennedy Street, Port Louis
Email: mauritius.embassy@dfat.gov.au Phone: +230 202 0160
Mauritius' official website is

mauritius.highcommission.gov.au.

Canada's High Commission

Contact: +230 202 9200 Email: prsls@international.gc.ca Address: c/o British High Commission, 2nd Floor, Rogers House, John Kennedy Street, Port Louis
Mauritius' official website is www.mauritius.gc.ca.

Please keep in mind that this information is subject to change, so it's best to double-check the contact information and operating hours of the respective embassies or consulates before visiting.

B. Travel Agencies and Tour Operators

Here are a few Mauritius travel agencies and tour operators:

Mauritius Travel Agency Ltd.

Address: 2nd Floor, One Cathedral Square, 16 Jules Koenig Street, Port Louis Contact: +230 212 6878 Website: www.mauritiustravelagency.com

Islandian

Contact: +230 202 6660 Address: 36 La Chaussée Street, Port Louis
Website: www.islandian.com

Mautourco Travel

Port Louis Waterfront, Caudan, Port Louis
+230 202 6666
Website: www.mautourco.com

Attitude Hotels

Royal Road, Calodyne, Grand Gaube
+230 209 9800 Website: www.attitudehotels.com

Emotions DMC Mauritius

Emotions DMC, Vieux Moulin, Rodrigues
+230 832 6900
Website: www.emotionsdmc.com

Beachcomber Tours

Address: 1, Bishop Paterson Avenue, Port Louis
Phone: +230 601 9000
Website: www.beachcombertours.uk

Mautourco Holidays Ltd.

Royal Road, Mont Choisy, Grand Baie
+230 209 8300
Website: www.mautourco.com

Tours with Ebrahim

9 Dr. Joseph Rivière Street, Port Louis

+230 212 6945

Website: www.ebrahimtours.com

Please keep in mind that this is not an exhaustive list, and it is recommended that you do additional research and read reviews before selecting a travel agency or tour operator. Furthermore, make certain that the chosen agency or operator is licensed and reputable.

C. Online Resources and Apps

Here are some online resources and mobile apps that may be useful to Mauritius visitors:

Official Website of the Mauritius Tourism Promotion Authority (MTPA): Mauritius' official tourism website offers information on attractions, accommodations, activities, and more. For more information, go to www.tourism-mauritius.mu.

Lonely Planet's Mauritius Travel Guide: This comprehensive travel guide app includes detailed information on attractions, restaurants, accommodations, maps, and more. iOS and Android versions are available.

Google Maps is a trustworthy navigation app with maps, directions, real-time traffic updates, and offline access. iOS and Android versions are available.

Moovit is a public transportation app that helps you navigate Mauritius' bus routes and schedules. It offers real-time bus arrival information as well as trip planning. iOS and Android versions are available.

Currency Converter XE: A currency conversion app that allows you to convert various currencies and obtain the most recent exchange rates. iOS and Android versions are available.

Weather Underground's Mauritius Weather Forecast: Get accurate and up-to-date weather forecasts for Mauritius, including temperature, humidity, wind speed, and more. iOS and Android versions are available.

TripAdvisor: A website that provides traveler reviews, recommendations, and booking options for Mauritius accommodations, restaurants, and attractions. iOS and Android versions are available.

Airbnb: A popular accommodation booking app that provides a wide range of options in Mauritius, including apartments, villas, and unique stays. iOS and Android versions are available.

Zomato: A restaurant, cafe, and eatery discovery app in Mauritius, with reviews, menus, and online reservations. iOS and Android versions are available.

Wi-Fi Finder: This app finds free Wi-Fi hotspots in Mauritius, making it easier to stay connected while traveling. iOS and Android versions are available.

Before using any app or online resource, make sure to read the reviews, ratings, and dependability. It's also a good idea to have offline maps and important information available in case of poor internet connectivity.

Printed in Great Britain
by Amazon

26570571R00106